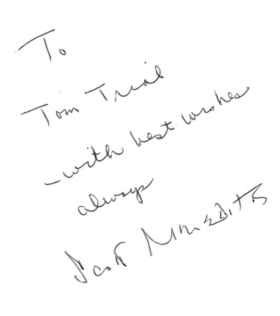

To

Tom Trial

— with best wishes

always

Scot Meredith

WRITING TO
SELL

Third Revised Edition

WRITING TO SELL

Scott Meredith

1817

HARPER & ROW, PUBLISHERS   New York
Cambridge, Philadelphia, San Francisco, Washington
London, Mexico City, São Paulo, Singapore, Sydney

Designed by Ruth Bornschlegel

Library of Congress Cataloging-in-Publication Data

Meredith, Scott.
    Writing to sell.

    Includes index.
    1. Authorship.   2. Fiction—Technique.   I. Title.
PN147.M48   1987   808′.02   86-45128
ISBN 0-06-015637-6

87 88 89 90 91 HC 10 9 8 7 6 5 4 3 2 1

To Helen, of course

Contents

*device: the "everything-remembered" script—How to make
long flashbacks more interesting*

*How much locale and background do books actually need?—
The proper way to paint in locale and background—Should
you ever skip locale and background entirely?—Locale in
big chunks, and locale in small doses—The use of the
senses in building locale—Should you write only
about things and places you know?—Foreign terms and
unfamiliar objects—How soon in a script must you
establish locale?*

Part Three: THE WRITING FACTS

*The ideal title—What the title must do for your book—How
much will a dull or trite title injure your sales chances?—
Editorial preferences in titles—The arty title—The misleading
title: love that sounds like murder—Proverbs and literary and
biblical quotations as titles—The grade-school–composition
title—Too-general titles—Incomprehensible titles—How to make
a trite title fresh by twisting it*

*Some light on the dark mystery of style—How style is
developed—Common errors of style, and how to avoid them—
The primary purpose and function of style—Overwriting
and its cure—The outstanding and easily recognizable style—
Rhythm in style: the mixture of long and short sentences—
The trick of underplaying—Why it makes scenes more effective*

*How to open a book—When to open a book—The just-before,
just-as, and just-after openings—The danger of too much*

*radio rights—Serial and anthology rights—How likely is it that
the publisher will reject your script after it's under contract?—
Royalties and the advance—The "self-destruct" clause—
When to consult an attorney—The attorney who
isn't a publishing specialist*

29.   Another Horizon: Nonfiction • • • *213*

*The major reasons for purchases and rejections—The opinion
book: when it will sell and when it won't—The
educational-helpful book—The problem of the
straight-educational book—The amusement-entertainment
book—The "you" appeal—The as-told-to book—
Big-name books and the small-town writer—Professional
attitudes in nonfiction writing*

30.   You're on Your Own • • • *219*

Things to remember when you begin the job of writing to sell

Introduction

by Arthur C. Clarke

The printed form that my secretary sends out in answer to ninety-five percent of my mail ends with these uncompromising words:

> So many publishers and authors have asked me to comment on books, or to write prefaces, that I am now forced to turn down *all* such requests, no matter how good the cause.

Now Scott Meredith jolly well *knows* this, for his office also sends out skillions of these forms in the hope of heading the mailman off at the pass. So what the heck am I doing here?

I'll tell you exactly how it happened. It began with a phone call to Scott from my dear friend (and fellow Meredith client) Isaac Asimov. "Scott," he said desperately, "I'm only 150 books ahead of Arthur—he's catching up. If you can slow him down just a bit, I'll give you the Lower Slobovian Second Serial Rights to *Asimov's Guide to Cricket*—without TV residuals, of course."

"Throw in that illustrated Braille *Kama Sutra* I know you're working on," Scott replied instantly, "and you have a deal."

"Done," said Isaac; whereupon Scott merely threatened to give my address to 589 people who want to know the real and secret message in *2001: A Space Odyssey,* and whether there'll be a sequel to *2010: Odyssey Two,* and here I am.... (There will be, incidentally. Scott recently negotiated and I've signed a contract for a book to be called *20001: The Final Odyssey.* Positively the final book in the series. I think.)

It was, for heaven's sake, a third of a century ago that Scott and I first met in person, as I stepped off the ocean liner (remember them?) onto the sacred concrete of Manhattan. At that time he looked about eighteen and wasn't *too* much older than that, and was thus only the second or third best literary agent in the United States; he was also still in a state of shock over the fact that he'd cabled to say that my book, *The Exploration of Space,* had just become a Book-of-the-Month Club selection, and I'd replied by asking innocently, "What *is* the Book-of-the-Month Club?" And it's quite a shock to me, so many years later, to look at the copyright page and realize that he had already written, and Harper had already published, the first edition of the volume you, gentle would-be writer, are now holding in your hands. . . .

Yet another shock, while we are about it. On going through what I laughingly refer to as my records, I've just discovered that it was nearly forty years ago that I sent Scott my first submission—the short story that later became the opening for *Childhood's End.* (See below.) I've long since forgiven him for insisting that it be rewritten; it probably needed it. . . .

It sometimes seems to me that every writer I know is represented by Scott, and acquired his basic skills as a staffer at Scott's agency. I'm exaggerating, of course; I *know* that Norman Mailer and Dr. Carl Sagan and Ernest K. Gann and Jessica Mitford and Gerald Green and hundreds of other Scott Meredith clients never worked for him. But he certainly seems to have had a hand in the beginnings and development of an apparently endless list of authors of present-day best-sellers. There's Harry Kemelman, for whose first novel, *Friday the Rabbi Slept Late,* Scott was only able to get an advance of $1,000, but went on to become a best-seller, and whose most recent contract—also, of course, negotiated by him—was for $500,000. There's Hank Searls, whose first sale via Scott was a short story to a now-defunct magazine for $50, and whose subsequent best-sellers include *Overboard,* a huge success, a selection of the Literary Guild, Reader's Digest Book Club, and four other book clubs, with the paperback rights selling for hundreds of thousands of dollars, a best-seller in a dozen other countries as well, and a motion picture. There's Robert Allen, whose first book, a little number called *Nothing Down,* received an advance of only $6,000, but went on to make millions, and who has since written another great best-seller, *Creating Wealth.* There's Dr. Stuart Mark Berger, a young physician whose *Dr. Berger's Immune Power Diet* became a #1 best-seller nationwide. There's also a young Englishman named Clarke who came to Scott in 1947 with that short story that Scott sold, as I recall it, for $70, and whose most recent novel was sold by Scott for—well, a bit more than that. And the list goes on and on.

Incidentally, Scott is no longer at 580 Fifth Avenue, his company address for twenty-six years, where I first met him; his agency has moved to larger quarters at 845 Third Avenue. However, the "scarred and lacerated spot on the wall" against which he beats his head from time to time, as mentioned in Chapter 27, has been carefully framed and moved to the new premises. When he is not using it, he pretends it's a Jackson Pollock on loan from the Metropolitan Museum of Art.

In all seriousness, I do not believe that *any* writer, however experienced he may fondly consider himself to be, could fail to benefit from this book. The fact that it is also highly entertaining doesn't do any harm; several times, I found myself laughing out loud. It says a good deal for Scott's sense of humor that it has survived so many decades of contact with authors . . . not to mention editors.

It would be impertinent of me to add anything to Scott's hard-won advice—so, I'll be impertinent.

It's always seemed to me that the biggest single problem any author has to face is: when should I give up? Scott would say, "Never!" and, as he describes in "Inspiration, Perspiration, Desperation," he has a special padded cell, equipped only with typewriter and a good supply of paper, in which he occasionally locks up authors to prove this theory. But it really isn't as simple as that.

Agreed, authors have an amazing capacity for inventing excuses not to work (Mine is a beautiful little monkey who cries piteously if not loved every hour, on the hour.) But there are times when no amount of staring at the typewriter and sweating blood will produce anything except frustration; you must learn to recognize those times.

Then you have two choices: you can switch to writing *something completely different* or, if that doesn't work, you must quit altogether. It was, I believe, Hemingway who said, "Writing is not a full-time occupation." That's true in more ways than one. You must live before you can write. And you must live *while* you are writing. But you mustn't kid yourself and make excuses to stop work by confusing laziness with the old standby "lack of inspiration." There is a lot of truth in the hard saying, "A professional can write even when he doesn't feel like it. An amateur can't—even when he *does.*"

The other big problem is to know when a job is finished. Sorry about all these quotations, but this is the most important yet: "No work of art is ever finished; it is only abandoned."

Old-time pros may snort indignantly at this; racing deadlines, they couldn't afford the time even for a second draft. Lester del Rey—another thoroughbred from the Scott Meredith stables, another staff editor at the agency who became and remains a Scott Meredith client, and now also, when he isn't writing, the guiding force of Del Rey Books, one of the very successful publishing companies that make up the Random House empire—could sit at the typewriter and produce, *within two hours,* a pretty good 6,000-word story. That's real professionalism, which I can only view with incredulous awe.

On another occasion, Lester sat down after breakfast and mailed off a 20,000-word novelette the same night. He admits that it might have been better if he'd left it until next morning . . . but would it have been all *that* much better? You can go on tinkering and revising and polishing forever; sometimes it is as hard to *stop* work on a piece as it was to start in the first place. But unless you're a poet turning out one slim volume every twenty years, you must learn to recognize the point of diminishing returns, and send your 99.99 percent completed masterpiece out into the cruel hard world. There's nothing wrong with amateurism (in the best sense of that misused word); but all serious artists are interested in money. And that means all *great* artists, too; take a look someday at Beethoven's correspondence with the London Philharmonic.

I'm in a generous mood this morning, possibly because of the $0.87 quarterly check I've just received for my five shares of COMSAT stock. So here, to give you inspiration, are a few ideas for books that I feel somebody ought to write. They cover a pretty wide range—biography, history, crime, science fiction, medical—with a couple of guaranteed best-sellers thrown in:

JONATHAN LIVINGSTONE SEA-SLUG

The inspirational saga of one of nature's humblest organisms, the adventurous Abominable Sea-Slug *(Mucus horribilis)*. Jonathan, born—or rather, fissioned—in a sewer outlet off Flushing, feels a dim impulse for higher things, and conceives the brave ambition of slithering upward to the glorious world above the waves. Unfortunately, despite the amazing camouflage that makes him almost indistinguishable from his surroundings, Jonathan is eaten by an even more revolting creature, the Squamous Scavenger-Fish *(Scatophagus vomitous),* before completing his odyssey.

SCREAMING FLESH

The memoirs of a famous surgeon, a pioneer of navel transplants, who is knighted by a grateful government when his revolutionary "brain bypass" operation transforms the fortunes of a political party. The author recalls, with brutal frankness and in loving clinical detail, carefree days as a young medical student in the Terminal Accident Ward at St. Sepulchre's. Though there are lighter moments—such as the hilarious episode of the electrified bedpans—sensitive readers may not get past Chapter 2, which gives the book its striking title.

SUNSET ON THE BOULEVARD

A moving account of the rescue work carried out by a rescue mission among the poor of Bel Air and Beverly Hills in the years following the Final Depression. There are harrowing stories of the destitute drinking the last drops of water in their swimming pools; maddened by hunger, trying to open Andy Warhol soup cans—and finally succumbing to fatal sunburn when the protective smog above Los Angeles vanishes.

DEFENDER OF THE DOOMED

The aptly titled autobiography of the famous criminal lawyer, whose courtroom exploits—hopefully—are never likely to be equaled. The author tells how he fought to save no less than ninety-eight clients from the gas chamber or electric chair—and lost them all. Now, for the first time, we learn exactly how he did it.

If you can't find something in *this* lot to trigger your imagination, perhaps you'd better stick to running your father's pre-stressed liverwurst business.

Just one minor point. Scott and I would *each* like ten percent of the loot.

And zero percent of the lawsuits.

PART ONE

THE BUSINESS
FACTS

YOU, WRITER
Your Place in the Writing Business

I am not, generally speaking, a betting man. But I am willing to wager a modest sum that there are, among those of you who have bought this book and are now reading these opening lines, a number who have been plagued with a feeling of worried perplexity ever since you plunked down the necessary amount on the bookstore counter. You've heard somewhere that writing ability is something with which you're born, like blue eyes or an upturned nose, and you're wondering whether or not trying to achieve literary success through study is a waste of money that might otherwise be spent on beer or ice cream sodas.

You'd be absolutely right, and I'd even go down with you and help talk the clerk into returning your money, if writing ability were the only requirement necessary in the building of a successful literary career. Basic writing ability is a product of many things, such as heredity, childhood reading, and personality, and neither this book nor any other can affect the question of Is you is or is you ain't a born writer. But writing ability is not the only requirement, not by a thousand miles.

To have basic writing ability and no technical knowledge, and to try to earn a living as a writer, is equivalent to finding yourself suddenly endowed with a large amount of steel, lumber, and bricks and, without any knowledge of architecture or building, setting out to earn your living building and selling houses. You might, by a fluke or by carefully examining houses that are already built, complete some that are approximately like professionally built houses, and even sell a few, but it is extremely unlikely that you will achieve any sort of major or lasting success at your work.

In the writing business, of course, there are a number of established authors who know nothing whatever about technique, and nevertheless manage to sell novels or nonfiction books or short stories or articles and go on selling them. Aside from the fact that these authors turn up about as often as quadruplets, which would make it downright silly for a new author to ignore technical study in the hope that he'll have the same kind of luck, it's interesting to note that these authors use, unconsciously, the same techniques that others with know-how use consciously. The psychological mystery of how these writers got this sense of structure isn't pertinent; the important thing is that there are definite methods in all kinds of writing, and you need them.

Let's assume, then, for the sake of getting some genuine good out of this book, that you do have basic writing ability, that you are a born writer. The chances are, anyway, if you've gone to the trouble of buying or borrowing this book, and intend to keep plugging away at writing no matter what I have to say in it, that the assumption is correct: because I've found again and again that the surest indication of the genuine writer is that amount of push and drive inside him that keeps him struggling to succeed at writing. His early scripts may not show it, and you sometimes have the feeling that the kindest thing would be to buy him a course in candymaking or welding, but if he keeps working away at it, you have the pleasure of watching his material change from terrible to fair to good to excellent.

With basic ability behind you, and the drive to keep at it, you probably want to know what other ingredients, aside from technical knowledge, you'll need to succeed. What, for instance, about education and cultural background?

The best way to discuss the former, I think, is to consider two of the best-known and most successful writers I represent, both of whom receive advances of well over $1,000,000 per book. One of them is a Harvard graduate; he holds a Phi Beta Kappa key and an M.A. degree. The other got as far as the eighth grade, when his father passed away, and he has had to work for a living ever since.

Go down any list of successful writers, and you'll find that the numbers of the educated and the not-so-educated are about equal. Personally, I don't believe that formal education or the lack of it makes a bit of difference either way. The important thing is that your education must be a good one, whether you've got a diploma to prove it or whether you've picked up your education through reading books or through friendships with intelligent, knowledgeable people.

In other words, you've got to be able to think and write clearly; you've got to have a reasonable familiarity with the English language, so that you can use the right words at the right times and achieve the effects you desire; you've got to know how to use your eyes and be reasonably observant of the things around you, because the darnedest objects, people, and occurrences pop up in your books and have to be described. It helps, of course, to be able to spell moderately well, and know how to use correct grammar, though these skills aren't terribly important. Many successful writers I know are worse spellers and grammarians than some of the kids I met back in the fourth grade; but they turn out first-class books and their wives or husbands or friends retype them and correct the errors.

The same, of course, applies to cultural background—whatever that may be—and travel experience: a great many writers eat lamb chops with their hands, are unable to swoon over a de Kooning however hard they try, and have traveled as far as two or three hundred miles in their lives.

The important reason that led to the fable that writers must be cultured and well-traveled, of course, lies in the fact that you must know something about people and places if you're going to write about them. If, however, as seems to be the case with most people who want to write, you're sensitive and perceptive about human relations, and learn a great deal through local observation and reading, there's no reason in the world to wait until you're sixty and understand Life, or to spend ten years roughing it along the upper Zambezi. Too often, the would-be writer's alleged wait for culture or "understanding" before he attacks the typewriter or word processor is a subconscious excuse for laziness or fear of failure.

The question of what you're going to write, now that we've made another assumption and decided that you have the necessary background along with your basic ability, is one that can be answered by asking yourself another question, and a very simple one: What do you like to read?

There used to be a very popular theory, now steadily lessening in popularity because it has been proved incorrect over and over again, that a writer must start by writing genre novels, such as mysteries or Gothics or Westerns, and that he should then set his sights on "better" goals by writing novels of the general or mainstream type, and then graduate, finally, to "literary" works. But this theory, which sounds perfectly logical until you examine it closely, fails because of one obvious fact: no man can do his best work at a job he dislikes. And in the writing business, you've always got to do your best work, because the competition, even in the lowest-paying markets, is tremendous.

In other words, a man whose favorite type of novel is strictly the general mainstream type can only delay his success by forcing himself to write, for example, science fiction novels.

In choosing *your* kind of writing, you've got to be absolutely honest with yourself, and concentrate on the kind of book you most like to read and would most enjoy writing. This does not mean the kind of book you'd like to tell your friends you're writing, or the kind of book at which your friends won't sneer; it means the kind of book you most like to read and write.

If you receive genuine enjoyment from the very literary, experimental, offbeat kind of book—and remember what I said about being honest with yourself: I am not referring to enjoyment of the awe in people's faces when you carry the book around with the cover showing—then that is the only kind of book for you to write. If you really enjoy the mainstream novel —the type that most often becomes a best-seller, like the books of Herman Wouk, Arthur Hailey, Ernest K. Gann, or James A. Michener—then that kind of book should be your specialty. And if you get the most pleasure out of one of the genres, like mysteries, then specialize in that type. The opportunities for success and for large income are equally good in any of the categories.

I've stressed the matter of selection of a type and specialization in that type because it is an important step that should be taken as early as possible in your career. Most writers find that they are naturally at home with one particular type, and this means that they probably will succeed most substantially in that area. In addition, the writer who vacillates between different types of novels may never become particularly proficient in any of them; and furthermore, if he does succeed in getting his novels in the different areas published, his varied appearances will not build for him the strong following he would get from the same number of novels concentrated in one field, because most readers prefer a single type of novel above all other types and give their allegiance to writers who supply them with that type. Think about the most successful writers of our time, and you'll find that, almost without exception, all of them specialize and write one type of novel. Choose your type, therefore, and though there's no harm in taking a busman's holiday once or twice if another type of book enters your mind and cries out to be written, stay with the chosen type most of the time.

I should mention, incidentally, that if you feel your first efforts will have a better chance for publication in paperback rather than hardcover, don't make the error of assuming that you may write badly or must write down. Although the writing may be a bit smoother, and the plotting and characterization a bit more careful in hardcover than in paperback, there truly isn't much difference between them. (I'll be elaborating on this in the next chapter.) You've got to write your best whichever type of book you choose, which is why you must choose a type to which you *can* give your best.

If, by the way, you start in a "lesser" field, such as genre paperback novels, and begin to succeed in it, you'll find that, despite any uneasy expectations you may have had, your relatives and friends won't sneer at you. No, writers for secondary fields are sneered at in generalizations, rarely face to face. There is something so impressive about the receipt of a check for a script, and the subsequent publication of that script, that the man who for years has sneered at, say, mysteries as trash will stumble all over himself to get to know you better if you have a check for a sale in your pocket, or a copy of your book with your name on the cover.

Once you've chosen your specialty, you'll want to decide whether you're going to sign your scripts with your own name or a pen name, for your byline is your trademark and a valuable property, and should be retained and built up with each script you sell. Generally, I advise new writers against the use of a pseudonym, and here's why:

There are several valid reasons why professional writers use pen names. For one thing, a writer's name doesn't always fit the type of fiction he writes: a writer of rough, tough, side-of-the-mouth detective novels may be unwilling to have them appear under his real name if his real name is Percy Harmondyne Whistlewillow. Women who write male-category material hide their sex under pen names; for example, B. M. Bower, Eli Colter, and Stewart Toland, all writers of Westerns—and all women. Some very prolific writers use pseudonyms in addition to their own names because they frequently have several books appearing at the same time, usually with different paperback houses, and they may want to avoid the impression that they are *too* prolific and that their books are being turned out too quickly.

Another reason may be that the author's name is foreign and unpronounceable and it is to his advantage to adopt a pleasant-sounding name that will be more easily remembered.

An example is Joseph Conrad, whose real name was Teodor Józef Konrad Korzeniowski. Still another reason may be that the author is writing about a subject that may get him in personal trouble, such as a book we recently sold that dealt with crooked politics and was based partially on fact. Its author, a resident of the city in which the book takes place, hid under a pseudonym because he might get his head kicked in if his identity were known. And one more reason is that a man may be writing part time until he sells steadily and becomes better established, and his job would be endangered if the boss found out he wasn't devoting his full faculties to the sale of more and more knitted ties.

All of these reasons are sound enough, but they are not in fact the reasons why most writers adopt pseudonyms. These are two-fold: "because people would kid me if they knew that I write" and "because I expect to improve as I go along and I don't want my early efforts to be held against me."

We've already, I think, disposed pretty thoroughly of the first reason. People may sneer at lesser-field writers in the abstract and people may grin at poor little Lois who thinks she can write books, but the sneers stop and the grins vanish when the books sell. And since your byline, whether pseudonym or real, would come before the public eye only in the event of a sale, it's muddy thinking to use a pseudonym for that reason.

The same principle applies to the second. A skill is bound to improve as you keep plugging away at it, whether the skill is writing or knitting or whistling through your teeth, and except in extremely rare cases of retrogression caused by such things as an increasing love for the contents of a whiskey bottle, most successful writers' first efforts don't compare to their later ones. You may be sure your early efforts won't be held against you. Quite the contrary, as a matter of fact: Your audience will like you better and better as they watch your books grow better and better.

If you have a valid reason for using a pen name, use one by all means. But don't use a pseudonym on the grounds of mistaken reticence or because you like to think of people wondering Who is the mysterious figure lurking behind the name of Herman Blugg? All you'll get out of *that,* as a top-selling novelist told me recently, is the frustrating experience of listening to your wife explain to people who are unaware that you write under a pen name why you stay at home all day like a bum instead of going out to work like decent people.

Make your choice intelligently but make it. The sooner you begin to build up your name, the sooner your name will mean more dollars per manuscript.

This book is a work on writing to sell, and my comments in this chapter have been concerned, as will all my comments in the chapters that follow, with commercial writing and placement for payment. It must be stressed, however, that these principles apply every bit as much to the work of so-called serious writers, who feel they are less concerned with writing for money than with contributing to the stockpile of the world's great literature.

The one thing the serious writer most often forgets, and which he should remember above everything else, is that almost no man on earth has ever succeeded in setting out deliberately to create a classic or masterpiece. Shakespeare, Zola, Dickens, Twain, and almost every other writer whose work has survived beyond his own generation, wrote—though without sacrificing his own literary values—entirely with the view of pleasing the current public and making money at it. Aside from the natural inner hope that every writer feels every time he writes, there was no deliberate, calculated attempt to create a centuries-surviving classic. They merely wrote the best manuscript possible and, because of the high quality of their work, and because they achieved enormous fame and popularity that was remembered past their generation, their books and plays became classics and are still enjoyed today.

A very few writers were unpopular in their own time and achieved a certain amount of attention afterward, but their later fame has been, generally, critical rather than popular. Shakespearean play productions are still sellouts today, and Dickens and Zola and Twain are still read and enjoyed by millions, but few of the critical-fame boys and girls are much read outside of required school study.

2

OFF ON THE RIGHT FOOT
Getting to Know the Market

What I have begun to do, in the preceding chapter, is to indicate the different types of novels—the genre novel, the mainstream novel, and the literary or experimental novel. In this chapter, we'll examine the ways in which the various types are published.

It used to be that any discussion of book markets had to focus on the difference between paperback and hardcover publishing, since there was a sharp division between the kind of material that sold first to paperback and the kind that sold first to hardcover. Hardcover publishers had a virtual monopoly on so-called quality material—the mainstream and literary novels—while the paperbacks were dominated by genre novels. Hardcover publishing's position had been set, of course, ever since the invention of the printing press. It wasn't until the 1940s that paperbacks appeared in force and began to take over from the all-fiction "pulp" magazines, turning out an immense variety and quantity of novels in all the popular genres. The line between hardcover and paperback was set, and the idea that hardcover meant quality and that softcover meant cheap entertainment was solidly established. In the eyes of most critics, the only paperbacks worth owning were those that weren't originals but were reprints of hardcover classics and best-sellers.

One key to the paperback business, until recently, was that low production costs and easy access to newsstand and bookstore rack space made it possible for the paperback firm to earn a profit even when a title had only modest sales. However, just as increased competition for rack space in the magazine field earlier destroyed the pulps and then many of the rest of the general-interest magazines, intense competition and increased costs are bringing about the demise of the modest-sale paperback. (Wholesalers and distributors today don't want to bother with a *lot* of paperbacks with sales of just forty or fifty thousand each; they prefer to concentrate on fewer and larger-selling titles.) The genre paperbacks that sell in small quantities for small profits are disappearing, because the fight for rack space, with a half-dozen books vying for each spot, has made this kind of publishing less and less successful. The old scheme of making a small profit per book on a lot of books, which added up to a good total profit, isn't working.

Paperback houses now are trying to make their money on fewer books, each of which sells bigger, and the only reason some of the larger and more famous houses continue to publish a lot of books monthly is to force out the little houses who have specialized in the small-quantity, small-profit book. When this process has run its course, the larger houses undoubtedly will accelerate the trend to fewer and bigger-selling titles.

The result of this, mentioned in the previous chapter, is that paperback quality has increased steadily to the point where the paperbacks are generally as good as the hardcovers. And the point of this, for you as a writer, is that, in most cases, you would be just as well advised to take your material to the hardcover firms as to the paperbacks, even in the popular genres.

Many newer writers still assume, if their work is in one of the genres—science fiction, mysteries, Westerns, romances, etc.—that their first efforts have a better chance for publication with the paperback houses than with the hardcover firms. But they're mistaken, since the decline of the modest-sale paperbacks means that the market for genre novels is actually stronger at hardcover than at paperback houses. The mystery, romance, or science fiction novel, when published as a paperback original, does not do nearly as well as a paperback reprint, which has had previous exposure in hardcover and which carries good critical reviews of the original hardcover edition on the cover or flyleaf. Readers are becoming more and more selective about the paperbacks they buy, particularly since paperbacks are no longer priced at fifty cents or a dollar but often cost twice as much these days as hardcovers used to cost. Readers generally will go for the paperback original in their favorite genre only if it seems to promise the kind of quality they would expect from a hardcover book. Keep in mind the fact that rising costs to publishers in paper, printing, binding, and all the rest have forced publishers to price both hardcovers *and* paperbacks so high that few people go into bookstores these days and make a casual purchase of a half dozen books that look interesting; book buying has become a thoughtful, measured activity where one tries hard to make sure that each book is enjoyed all the way through rather than tossed across the room in disgust after the first chapter.

So we've established that no matter what kind of novel you write, there are at least two good reasons why you should aim for hardcover: the difference in quality between hardcover and paperback is disappearing, and the hardcover markets are stronger than those for "paperback originals." And if you do achieve hardcover publication, this means that you're in a position to reap another and even more important advantage— because that hardcover breakthrough means a highly increased opportunity for income. Advances against royalties for first novels aren't so different between paperback and hardcover—they average between $2,500 and $10,000. But hardcover publication offers a far greater chance for subsidiary income from motion picture, serialization, and foreign sales, because movie companies, magazine editors, etc., are, to put it bluntly, more impressed with hardcover books than paperback originals and tend to buy them more often. (They shouldn't be, necessarily, but—let's face it—they are, so much so that many agents offer movie rights to forthcoming paperback originals in manuscript so that potential buyers won't know immediately that the book they're considering is going to be published only in paperback. It's only after the buyer becomes deeply interested that the agent tells him the book is a forthcoming paperback original.) Then, of course, on a hardcover book, there's subsequent money from the paperback reprint. And the advertising and bookstore-display advantages that can accompany hardcover publication increase the chances that your book will be a hit and your career will get a successful start.

On that matter of paperback reprint, incidentally, there are two ways in which this can happen. One is what has become known in the publishing industry as the hard/soft deal, which is an arrangement with one of the increasing number of hardcover publishers who also own or are otherwise associated with a paperback house, and which is essentially a dual deal under which the hardcover publisher brings out its edition first, and then, when sales have slowed down or stopped, the paperback edition comes out. The other is the more conventional arrangement, with a hardcover house that has no paperback affiliation, in which the hardcover publisher contracts only for its own edition but also controls the paperback rights, and licenses an unaffiliated paperback house to publish an eventual softcover edition, for which the hardcover publisher receives a share of the paperback revenue. Back in the darker days of publishing, the rigid and unchangeable rule was for the hardcover publisher and the author to share equally in that revenue, fifty percent apiece, but that has now changed, and it's sometimes possible these days to negotiate a 60/40 share in favor of the author, and occasionally even a 70/30 share or better.

At the present time, there are a lot of hardcover publishers with paperback affiliations, and vice versa. As this is written (and I use that phrase because publishing affiliations tend to shift and change rapidly), Doubleday, for example, owns a paperback house, Dell; Random House owns three paperback houses, Ballantine, Fawcett, and Del Rey; Putnam's parent house, MCA, owns three paperback houses, Berkley, Jove, and Ace; Simon and Schuster owns Pocket Books; NAL, a paperback house, has bought a hardcover house, Dutton; Hearst, the parent of two hardcover companies, Morrow and Arbor House, also owns a paperback company, Avon; Macmillan, a hardcover house, has just signed an agreement to publish twenty-five books in association with a paperback house, Warner; and so forth. In general, and when you can get it, a hard/soft arrangement is a better deal because of two things: you can generally get a larger amount of money up front—a bigger advance—because you're arranging simultaneously for two types of publication, and two companies or two divisions of the same company are each pouring funds into the pot, and also because, in many hard/soft deals, the hardcover publisher doesn't take a share of the paperback money but lets all paperback earnings go to the author, having made an arrangement with his paperback partner to give him an "override" of some royalty money as his compensation. The conventional deal with a hardcover publisher alone, however, also has its advantages, since the hardcover firm is not locked in to a specific paperback arrangement, and, if a book it publishes becomes a great success, it can then auction paperback rights among all the paperback publishers and perhaps make so huge a deal that the author will benefit even though the hardcover publisher takes a share of that money. For that reason, it's important to examine each situation carefully and try to determine the potential of the book involved, in order to make the right choice; but, whether it's hard/soft or conventional, it's best to go for hardcover publication first.

All this advice about the advantages of hardcover publication may puzzle you if you've heard the talk in recent years about the enormous success of the larger paperback houses and the decline of some of the hardcover firms. These reports of the rise of paperbacks are quite true, but if you'll go back to the original newspaper and magazine stories and reread the accounts of fabulous sums paid by the paperbacks, you'll find, virtually without exception, that the sums were paid for paperback rights to a book that had already been established as a best-seller in hardcover. Although a few of the large paperback houses have begun challenging the hardcovers by commissioning original novels by top authors, this really amounts to nothing more or less than hardcover publishing in softcover form, and doesn't alter the fact that paperback firms, by and large, need the hardcover publisher to get the title off the ground. And, in most cases, so will you.

The upshot of this discussion is that no matter what type of book you write—genre novel, mainstream novel, juvenile novel, or experimental—there is basically just one type of market for your work. There is no need to "slant" your writing toward hardcover or paperback; there is simply a need to do the very best work you can do within the particular type of writing you choose.

We'll be talking mostly about writing novels in this book, since the disappearance of so many magazines has led to severe shrinking of the magazine market, but nearly everything said here about the techniques of writing and selling novels applies to short fiction, too. And in many of the chapters later in the book, particularly those dealing with idea-getting and plotting and style and other aspects, I'm going to show that the basic facts and rules are the same whichever type of fiction you choose. It is essential, however, that you pick your field early, so that your general technique may be curved and bent to meet the specific requirements of that field. And this choice, I trust, you have now made.

3

THE CURRENT SITUATION
What Editors Buy

Today's book market is so wide open for new ideas—new kinds of themes, new types of characters and writing styles, and crossbreeds of genres—that it makes more sense to list the things that editors tend to reject than to talk about what they purchase. The variety of material considered appropriate grist for the literary mill is endless, and is expanding every day as our society becomes more open to examining all aspects of life. There are very few taboos left in the book publishing business.

The restrictions that do exist are not, by and large, taboos related to morality, but practical considerations concerning what will and what will not sell to the intelligent book-buying public. For example, most publishing houses will not take kindly to a novel of less than, say, 45,000 words, for the cold-blooded business reason that production and printing of the short novel will cost nearly as much as a longer, more standard-size novel, which means that the retail price of the book will have to be just about the same, but many book shoppers will resist paying the standard price for such a slim volume. Our increasingly cost-conscious consumers of books like to feel that they're getting a lot for their money; hence the rise of such trends as the "queen-size" Gothic novel of around 90,000 words, and the even longer and more elaborate historical Gothics.

Of course, there are notable exceptions to this rule about length—*Love Story, Jonathan Livingston Seagull,* and others —but then, there are no absolute restrictions in the publishing world.

Another nonabsolute rule is the one against a novel that's too long. It may sound funny, but whether or not a script is too long is not simply a matter of its length. What counts is whether or not the book is too long for its story and what it has to say—whether, in other words, the reader can be held and induced to keep flipping the pages until the end. The "standard" length for novels is from 60,000 to 100,000 words, but a 60,000-word novel can be too long if it's really nothing more than a long-winded telling of an incident (more on that in a later chapter), and a 250,000-word novel can be just right if the story and characters truly need that much length and if the reader can remain happily absorbed until the end.

Generally speaking, there tend to be stronger restrictions on length in the genre novels than in the other categories, largely because genre editors feel that only so many pages can be devoted to the solution of a murder, or the completion of a cattle drive, or the rescue of a space station, before the fan and reader of that particular genre will begin to feel that he's being loaded down with a lot of stuff he didn't want. Exceptions to this are books like the long historical Gothic, mentioned earlier, and the occasional science fiction or fantasy epic in which the world projected by the author is so unique, and so filled with mind-boggling implications, that the readers can't seem to get enough.

The important thing to remember about your script's length is that if you plan to write one of the exceptions to the rules—if you're writing, say, a mainstream novel of only around 40,000 words, or a mystery of more than 100,000 words —your work, in order to overcome editorial skepticism, may have to be considerably better than if you had aimed for a more conventional length.

Although there are optimum limits on your script's length, every other aspect of book manuscript buying is characterized by an absence of rules. Almost no theme, for example, is automatically unacceptable, unless it is in poor taste or unless it is too trite. Poor taste would include themes advocating genocide, racial bias, and the like.

Excessively trite themes mar reading enjoyment enough to become taboo, too. You'll have a hard time selling, for example, books in which the chief problem is the paying off of the mortgage or the company debt, or wherein the obstacle to the marriage is the stern father with his inevitable questions about the hero's financial future. Taboos in Westerns, to give another example, include the overtrite story of the lone cowhand who wanders onto the ranch from which cattle are being rustled, and gets the rancher's daughter and the foreman's job when the foreman turns out to be the thief. Editors also tear their hair out these days over scripts in which heroines are described by the trite device of having them look into mirrors and observe each of their features. (This sort of thing: "She looked for a long moment in the mirror, admiring her long taffy-colored hair, her dark eyes, her straight little nose, and the way her smooth shoulders shone against the strapless black gown. She knew the new boy would like her." Sickeningly familiar, isn't it?)

There is more and more demand among editors and readers for more original and meaningful themes in all types of fiction, including the genre novel. For example, mystery novels that show the hero searching personally for the murderer are now likely to show him looking simultaneously for the answer to some personal problem. Science fiction novels that project civilizations of the future are likely to present a civilization with parallels relevant to the pressing problems of our own society. In adventure novels, there is no longer action for action's sake, or even justice for justice's sake; the characters must have a personal, meaningful stake in what they're doing. And in juvenile books, there is no longer any room for scripts of the Who Killed Cock Robin? variety; the trend is toward realism and personal relevance in every area.

Similarly, characters are no longer wanted who are either

unbelievably heroic or too stereotyped. They should be real to the reader, with qualities, problems, concerns, and feelings with which the reader can identify. This does not mean that characters should be dull or bland or exactly like the boy or girl next door. Your main characters should be believable but individualized, so that the editor won't feel that he's met them in a few dozen other books.

One of the questions most frequently asked by newer writers is whether they should go ahead and complete their script, so that editors can consider it in its entirety, or whether they'd be better off submitting a "portion-and-outline," a script consisting of some initial chapters plus an outline of how the book will continue and end. Many established professionals submit a portion-and-outline regularly instead of a completed script, and the practice saves them a lot of time.

The rationale given by many newer writers who want to use a portion-and-outline is that they're afraid that writing the entire script will prove to be a waste of time if no editors like it. But the danger is that often this is just another one of those ingenious excuses writers invent to stave off the rigors of completing a script. Early in your career, before you've made a major sale, you'll need the experience and discipline of writing the entire script. And another compelling reason for writing the whole book is that editors often hesitate to buy a portion-and-outline from an unknown writer; they have no evidence that the new writer will be able to do a satisfactory job of completing the work he's started.

However, a portion-and-outline can be a fine idea when you're already established or when you just want to do enough, for example, to get your editor's or agent's opinion on the salability of your idea and approach. If you do decide to work with a portion-and-outline, make sure that you include enough completed material to give the reader an adequate idea of your handling of the script—at least fifty pages, in most cases. Your outline should be matter-of-fact in describing the plot; don't try to oversell the outline with explanations of why you decided on particular plot developments or with your interpretations of the meanings of the plot events. As in the rest of the script, let the characters and their actions speak for themselves.

4

THE INSIDE STORY
Behind Editorial Doors

At least one book in every hundred offered to editors contains a page that is upside down or two pages that are stuck together at one corner with a light dab of glue. This is an ancient wheeze coined around 1850—although many new writers using it believe they've just invented the idea—and it is designed to determine whether or not the editor has read the script if it is returned, rejected, with the page still reversed or the two pages still stuck together.

You may take my word for it that there's no real point in such subterfuge for, with exceptions so very rare that they're not worth worrying about, every script submitted to a publishing house is read—or, at least, enough of it is read to determine whether or not it should be bought or returned. (Experienced editors can sometimes tell that a script isn't for them after they've seen the first two chapters or even the first two pages.)

It's frustrating to realize that the script over which you've labored so hard may not be read beyond the first chapter when you offer it for sale, and it's frustrating to get it back with a printed rejection slip or brief form note, which gives you no clue to the reasons for rejection, but the fact is that editors are extremely busy men and women whose only reason for looking at the script at all is the hope that they can publish it. If a quick look or a full reading assures them that they cannot, they toss it aside and hurry on to the next script. They can afford to take time to write a long letter only when they believe a script can be fixed up and made purchasable or when a script isn't right that time but the author is sufficiently close that he may make the grade next time.

At dinner recently, a well-known editor told me about the problems he encountered when he started in his job.

"I suppose that what happened to me has happened to every editor just starting out," he said. "When I first arrived at the office, I was going to read every script thoroughly and write a helpful critique to the author of each script I rejected. Like many others in the business, I'd done some writing myself, and I knew how a stock rejection, after five weeks of waiting, could make you feel like jumping off the highest available bridge. I had about thirty scripts to read when I got to the office." He shook his head. "I'd read two of them thoroughly by the middle of the next morning, when another dozen scripts were delivered to me. When I realized that I had to take care of a thousand other things that day—like talking with the art director about covers, helping to plan ad campaigns for some of our books, meeting with an author whose agent had submitted a sensational first novel, and then meeting with an agent who wanted better terms for one of our established authors—I knew I was going to have to find a different way to handle the reading of scripts.

"I felt like a traitor at first," the editor said, "but I had no choice. I took the first script on the pile and started reading as fast as I could. When I'd seen enough to know that it wasn't right, I just tossed it on the rejection pile and started right in on the next script."

Let's suppose, as happens far more frequently than you might think, an editor looks over a submission and sees that it's a mystery novel when his firm doesn't happen to publish mysteries. There's no reason in the world for him to read that script thoroughly; all he has to do is give it a quick look and see if it's so sensational that he ought to publish *that* mystery, and reject it if it isn't. Let's suppose that he realizes after reading the first chapter that a script is too clumsily written or plotted for purchase, or that it is based on a subject that has been done to death in the current market, or that, in short, the script—for any reason whatever—is one he cannot buy or have the author fix. He won't read *those* scripts all the way through; his time limits and the press of other business won't let him. He will, however, read a close-but-not-quite script all the way through, perhaps read some sections twice, before turning it down, and he'll always try to write a little note of encouragement to an author who is close—for the simplest business reason that he must have good books to make a successful list. Sometimes he's so rushed with other work that there's no time even for little notes of encouragement; he just sends the script back and hopes the author will keep plugging until he makes the grade.

Because of time tightness, most publishing houses work on a two-pile system consisting of the rush pile and the unrush or slush pile. Under this method, all scripts that arrive are sorted before reading into two groups. Into the rush pile go scripts by authors who have been published by the house in the past, scripts by authors who have not been published by that house before but are well known, and scripts submitted by good agents. Scripts by new writers who are recommended by established authors also usually go into the rush pile. The unrush or slush pile draws scripts by unfamiliar names and scripts submitted by new agents who are unknown to the editor.

The rush pile, for obvious business reasons, gets the first and fastest reading, because the editor knows he has a better chance to get publishable books from it. Published authors and agents from whom he buys regularly can usually be expected to turn up with good stuff. Rush-pile buying is heavy.

Subsequently the editor turns to the unrush pile and here the buying is lighter. Many scripts as described, get the quick brush-off: they obviously aren't right. Others are read and put aside for later rereading; they aren't quite right but perhaps the author can fix them up or perhaps they should be rejected and the author encouraged to try again. And others are read and put aside as scripts the editor likes and wants to recommend for publication at the next meeting of the editorial board.

There used to be a legend that some editors would reject a

perfectly publishable first novel but solicit further submissions in order to determine whether or not the author was consistent and could be depended upon to provide the house with many books instead of just one. Nonsense. Editors desire consistency in an author, of course, because they're hoping for a long and successful relationship, but they're not going to risk rejecting a good book and see a rival publishing house snap up the author.

Besides, purchase of books by new writers is important for three good reasons. For one thing, new writers' scripts may be purchased at minimum advances, which helps balance the budget and fit in higher-priced books by name writers. For another, new writers are needed to replace established authors who have died, or moved to other fields, and they frequently turn out to be as good as, or better than, the established authors in the field. And finally, editors who discover new writers who become established authors bolster their own reputations and make their own jobs additionally secure.

It's only at the smallest houses that a single editor reads both the rush and the unrush piles. At most houses a group of assistant editors and readers reads the unrush, while the senior editors read the rush and those scripts selected from the other pile by the readers or assistants. The scripts that the senior editors like then generally go before an editorial board, usually composed of all senior editors plus the head of the firm, and sometimes including the firm's sales manager and advertising manager, for final okay.

These mass-approved setups frequently horrify writers, who fear that their book's chances of acceptance are reduced by the necessity of being passed by a number of different people. Actually this fear is almost groundless. Senior executives at a publishing house generally look for the same kinds of books on the same quality levels, and a script that one experienced editor likes will usually be liked by all the other men and women on the staff.

There's one other relatively recent development in the publishing field which I'd better mention (if you haven't heard about it previously, though it's gotten a lot of publicity and you probably have) because it's important, even though it will distress you because it's one more roadblock in the path of the writer trying to break in, and a big one. That is the new policy of many publishing houses not to consider unsolicited manuscripts (meaning submissions by people other than major agents and established authors) at all, and it's a policy that seems to be spreading every month.

Actually, this all began quite a long time ago, in the heyday of the original *Saturday Evening Post* (not the current clone of the same name), when the *Post* was still a weekly and paid the highest prices in the business for serials, novelettes, short stories, and articles. But the prominence of the *Post* as a market brought it a huge number of submissions, requiring a similarly huge staff of readers, and one day the magazine's executives, alarmed at the size of the company payroll, decided to do an internal survey to determine whether or not all the cost and effort was repaid via the discovery of a sufficiently large number of publishable scripts in the slush piles. The executives suspected that that might not prove to be the case, but the results startled them. They discovered that, of the last three thousand scripts they'd bought and published, only *two* had come off the slush pile; the other 2,998 had come from agents and similar sources. So the next move was immediate and obvious: the *Post* dismissed most of its reading staff, announced that it would no longer consider unsolicited manuscripts, and added blandly that it was just going to allow the agents to undertake the job (and the costs) of being the talent seekers and discoverers.

Since then, more and more publishers, particularly book publishers, have come to the same conclusion, that the cost of being discoverers just isn't worth it, since they buy almost entirely from agents anyway, and the agents will do the discovering for them. And these aren't the minor publishing firms, either; among the firms that have announced that they'll only consider manuscripts from agents and established authors are Doubleday, Simon and Schuster, Random House, Harper & Row, Dutton, and Morrow.

The result is that when you send a script to one of these firms these days, you get the script back with a printed form stating they no longer consider unsolicited material and enclosing, sometimes, a list of the names and addresses of agents, either a selected list of the agents with whom the company does most business or a reprint of the list of agents in the Manhattan telephone directory yellow pages.

Obviously, this isn't a benevolent attitude or the old-style publishing ambition of trying to search out the best, but publishers today maintain that it's a necessity because, with printing and paper and binding and shipping and overhead costs already so high, the costs of continuation of a script-hunting program they don't really need would move the prices of books that final mile out of the reach of most bookstore patrons (and it's close to that level already). For the man or woman trying to make it as a writer, of course, it's a rough situation, particularly since, as you'll hear people grumbling all the time, it's just as hard to get an agent as a publisher, if not harder. This isn't too far from the truth. Young actors feel frustrated when they find that they can't get work without a union card but can't get a union card without work credits. So writers are often faced with the situation where they write to agent after agent who won't even consider their scripts unless and until they have an impressive sales record but never explain about how writers are supposed to get those sales if more and more publishers won't even consider their work unless it comes via an agent. There are really only two solutions to this truly difficult dilemma. If you want to work through an agent, either because you feel an agent can do a better job of selling and negotiating than you can do yourself, or because the publisher you'd like to have for your book is one of the firms that bars unsolicited submissions, then you've just got to write to a lot of agents and keep writing until you get one, because, fortunately, there *are* still agents around who'll consider the work of unestablished writers, though some charge a fee to cover their costs in doing so. If you want to submit directly to publishers, there are, again fortunately, still many publishers who don't have the locked-door policy. A good guide like *Literary Market Place*, which is available at most larger public libraries and is published by the firm that also publishes the weekly bible of the industry, *Publishers Weekly*, lists all reliable publishers and agents, together with their addresses, phone numbers, and other pertinent information.

When a book is cleared for purchase, the editor immediately contacts you or, if you have one, your agent, to settle the major terms of the purchase contracts. These usually center around the amount of the advance against royalties, the royalty schedule, the specific rights you convey to the publisher or retain (there's a chapter on rights and contracts later on). If the entire manuscript has been submitted and approved, the advance against royalties will customarily be payable in full upon signing of contracts, although some houses may split the advance, with half to be paid upon signing and the other half to be paid upon publication of the book. If you have submitted a portion of the book and an outline of the rest, half of the advance usually is paid upon signing and the remainder paid upon delivery and acceptance of the full script. After the contracts have been approved and signed by author and publisher, a voucher for the appropriate amount of the advance is filled out and sent to the accounting department. Where the firm has an involved disbursement system, or where the disbursement system *could* be rapid but the man who pays always has to wrestle with himself for a while before he shells out, you or your agent will sometimes receive the completed contracts first and the check a week or two later. When you do have an agent, incidentally, the publishing house always returns two copies of your contract, one for your files and one for your agent's.

Copies of the manuscript are then made, and the original is placed in the editorial safe or library. A few copies are given to the copy editors, who mark the script for the printers, and the book is soon scheduled for publication, usually for sometime at least six months ahead in hardcover publishing and at least four months ahead in paperback. A copy of the script is also given to an artist or design group for a cover. The printers then publish in three stages. First they print the book in long sheets, which are called galleys. After these have been proofread and corrected, the galleys are cut into page size; these sets, which are sometimes bound with a soft cover and resemble a paperback book, are called the page proofs and are given a final check prior to publication. And finally the book comes out and shows up at your local bookstore, where you have been camping for months.

It's a good idea to drop the editor a brief letter thanking him for buying your script and, later, thanking him for the check (unless the sale was made by an agent, in which case he'll be sure to thank the editor for you), but this does not mean an eight-page affair detailing your struggles in the writing business. The publishing house, especially if it is a hardcover firm, will send you a questionnaire in which you provide the publicity department with information about yourself and your career.

As for the letter to send when you're offering your script, make it as brief and businesslike as possible. If the submission is your first novel, or if this would be your first sale, then tell the editor so, and say little else; if you've had previous sales, that information should be included. Don't tell the editor how the idea for the book came to you while you were polishing your shoes, or how you write just like Norman Mailer, only better. Don't try to sell the script in your letter. Let your work do the talking.

Fully ninety percent of the letters accompanying new writers' submissions state nothing more, when analyzed, than the fact that the writer is submitting herewith a script, but it's sometimes said interminably. If that's all you have to say, say it in ten words, not in four hundred. If the editor's eyeglasses are good enough to enable him to see at all, they are good enough to enable him to see that you've sent him a script, not an elephant or a hard-boiled egg.

Anything that may get you on the rush pile or increase your chances of acceptance is certainly adequate reason for writing a longer letter. The former is quite possible, so by all means remind the editor that you've had five stories in major magazines even though this is your first book, or that Arthur Hailey suggested you send the script and an introductory letter from Hailey will be arriving shortly. The latter—increasing your chance of acceptance—is practically impossible; don't try it unless you are able to remind the editor that you are his wife's adored kid brother, or that you happen to have a picture of him with a blonde at "21" when his wife thought he was working late, or that your father happens to be president of the bank at which he has just requested a personal loan. These are the only three cases that can favorably increase the chances of a script's sale; otherwise, unless you have some specific background, as described, that will get you on the rush pile, don't write a letter at all.

And don't, whatever you do, enclose a letter instructing the editor to purchase the book because you have seen far worse published by his company. This will bring your script home promptly, possibly accompanied by a lighted stick of dynamite.

Aside from the obvious diplomatic error in informing an editor that he occasionally publishes rotten books or that he usually publishes rotten books, the chances are more than excellent that you may be wrong. You may, for one thing, not be experienced enough to judge whether or not a book is good, especially in the sense of whether or not a particular audience will like it. You may, for another, never become experienced enough, for it is a truism of this business that many excellent writers are never able to evaluate correctly another writer's work or, for that matter, their own.

When one very well-known client brings in a new novel and

raves about it, I can usually be sure it will be a dud; when he brings in a new script with a glum or apologetic look on his face, it usually receives public acclaim. I know a hundred other writers with the same knack for prophecy in reverse.

On submissions to a publishing house, by the way, you should have a report in four to seven weeks, exclusive of mail travel time. The latter wait is typical for scripts on the unrush pile. If more than the normal length of time passes without a report, don't assume that the publisher is interested; it may mean nothing more than the fact that there have been several illnesses or vacations or firings in the editorial department.

Your best bet, any way you look at it, is to force yourself to forget a script the moment it is put into the mail and concentrate on writing new material. You'll know what has happened to it when you find the publisher's offer in your mailbox.

5

INSPIRATION, PERSPIRATION, DESPERATION
Working Habits

The writing life looks easy to the nonwriter. All you have to do, he says, eyeing you enviously, is sit down at a typewriter every once in a while and pound out a script and go collect a big check for it. No time clocks; no bosses; no one to tell you what to do and when to do it.

The working writer, however, knows that the job of pounding out that script is anything but easy, particularly after he has passed the beginner's stage, where any careless mass of wordage he has produced looks good to him, and he has begun to work in the professional, planned way that produces salable material. He also knows that the complete lack of time clocks and bosses in the writing business, in addition to being its most wonderful aspect, can frequently be its biggest headache.

When a bookkeeper comes to the office and doesn't feel much like keeping the books that day, he keeps them anyway because he knows the boss will bawl him out or fire him if he is caught sitting around reading a magazine. As a result, the work gets done. The full- or part-time writer, however, is his own boss in his writing work, and too often the work does not get done.

Through the years, writers have invented a multitude of excuses and delaying actions to avoid settling down to the job of turning out that salable script, with their chief ally the conclusion that writing is a delicate mental undertaking that can easily go awry if conditions are not exactly right. Among the devices employed are the wait for inspiration, the presence of that picture on the wall that is crooked and will distract if it isn't straightened, the necessity for sharpening those blunt pencils (even though you type your stuff and practically never use the pencils), the lack of a really suitable hideaway in which to write, the fact that you were out late the previous night and your mind isn't as clear and sharp as necessary, the fact that you had a hard day at the office and your stuff won't receive full justice if you undertake your spare-time writing stint that evening, the noise your family or the neighbor's children are making, and the conviction that the writing just doesn't seem to be coming right that day so what's the sense in continuing? There are about a hundred others; if you have a writer's active imagination, you'll think them up yourself.

Well, your friends and family aren't listening right now, so let me state it bluntly: most of these are just as make-believe as that fiction you write.

If you will force yourself to work out those book ideas without waiting for inspiration to slosh you across the back of the head, and if you will force yourself to write one sentence after another despite the fact that the picture is awry, and the pencils are blunt, and your family is making an awful racket, and you're writing in one corner of a bedroom instead of in a big soundproof study, and you had a big night with the boys last night, and the stuff looks awful as you write it—you will find, when you examine it a day or two later, that the material you've produced is exactly as good or bad as the material you normally produce, or would produce under ideal conditions.

Naturally, you will do good work on some days and not-so-good work on others; science is constantly seeking to discover —though it has not yet succeeded—why people in every trade and profession do excellent work at certain times and not-so-excellent work at others. The important thing is that the excuses upon which writers so often seize to avoid work usually have very little to do with it. If you keep a careful checklist, you will find, as years pass, that some of your best work was produced under working conditions that were very poor, and that some of your worst material was written while you were working under conditions that were absolutely ideal.

The best cure for the habit of literary procrastination, and the best way to avoid the habit if you have not yet fallen into it, is the stern and rigid working schedule: the setting of specific hours during which you must sit and write. If you do this, and abide strictly by the schedule, you will get your work done because you are forcing yourself to be as tough a boss to yourself as a boss in a standard business is to his employees.

Many new writers are shocked at the notion of a writing schedule, and feel they simply can't write that way. This is usually just another subconscious excuse and it can usually be dismissed by a little honest self-questioning and a little logic. After all, when you get right down to it, why can't you? When you attend school, you're under a rigid schedule: you begin work at a specific hour and stop work at a specific hour and work steadily during those hours. When you have a job, you begin and end at set times and work with reasonable steadiness in between. And if you're married and your job is homemaking, you still work on a fairly rigid schedule, preparing the meals and cleaning and doing the other household chores at specific times.

It adds up exactly the same way, except that in school and as an employee, you have teachers and truant officers and bosses to watch over you, and as a housewife, there are the children and your husband to complain if the meals aren't ready on time or if the clothes aren't kept mended and clean. You're on your own as a writer, and you'll get your work done if you set up that harsh boss, the religiously followed schedule to keep you working hard.

When you set up a schedule, don't go overboard with it. It's designed to keep you working hard, but not so abnormally hard that you can't possibly keep up with it for long. Set it so that you get in as much work as you can handle, not any more and not any less. If you're a part-time writer, two or three hours an evening about three evenings a week is plenty; more than that will make your combined jobs so great a strain on your physical and mental health that you soon won't be able to do either. If you're a full-time writer, then from nine or ten o'clock to five, five days a week, with an hour off for lunch, is more than adequate.

All things considered, there is only one kind of writer who should not use the schedule system: the writer who discovers, after extended tryouts of both systems, that he really gets more work done by going to the typewriter at unspecified periods, and who is a good enough self-disciplinarian to spend plenty of total time at his typewriter. If you find that you are really in this small group—and make sure you aren't just talking yourself into it to get away from a tough boss—go ahead and work that way.

Otherwise, stick to a schedule, and force yourself to write steadily during the hours you have set for yourself. You'll find that regular writing will turn into a habit, and that's a wonderful thing.

Motion pictures and television frequently depict writers as hard-drinking men, and sometimes as comic drunks. There's nothing comic about it. Too many writers have risen high in their profession and then sunk back into failure because of their overfondness for patronizing the package stores.

I said a little while ago that you needn't fear to work the morning after a big evening with the boys, and that still goes. If you're reasonably normal, your mind isn't so weak that a frolicsome night will make it function fuzzily enough to impair the quality of your stuff. The mental fuzziness that comes from habitual drinking, however, is another matter entirely.

When you begin to hit the bottle too regularly, you can kiss your writing career good-by and reserve a hallway in Skid Row for sleeping purposes. I don't know why many new writers believe they must drink heavily as part of their chosen profession; perhaps it is because writing is a romantic trade, and some of them think there is also something romantically disreputable and free thinking about being the hard guy or dame who drinks. Perish that thought: your colleagues in the adjoining beds of the drunk wards will number some of the weakest-minded and least romantic individuals in your city.

Most important, don't ever drink at all—not even an eye-dropper's worth—when you're working, particularly if you ever get the bright idea of doing so to speed up your thinking or writing. You'll speed up at first, all right, but after a while you'll find yourself having to drink more and more to be able to write less and less. Soon you won't be able to write at all without drinking; and a little later you won't be able to write at all.

The same applies to stay-awake pills and all other artificial stimulants. You're better off staying away from them entirely, and certainly while you're writing. Most writers have made their way through the stimulus of their natural abilities, and so can you.

Sometimes, when you have left an incomplete scene or chapter alone for a while, you will return to it to find that it has cooled off. You just can't seem to get started again; you just can't seem to return to the mood.

There are several professional tricks designed to prevent an occurrence of this sort, and to combat it if it does happen. The best of these is one that works to keep it from happening at all.

When you're hot in the middle of a scene or chapter and you note the arrival of your schedule end or the time you have been planning to quit, the natural tendency is to keep working as long as things are going so well. It's natural, but it may be a mistake. Stop right there—right in the middle of a sentence, or even in the middle of a word.

When you keep going until you finish the scene or sequence on which you're working, the job before you next time is almost equivalent to that of starting an entirely new script. You've got to make a fresh beginning with a new scene, and it isn't surprising if you find it hard to do when you next come to your type-writer. When you stop in midsentence or midword, however, your mind has already preceded you—and you know just what you have to write. You sit down at the typewriter or word processor and finish the word, sentence, and paragraph, and you can usually swing on from there into the rest of the script.

If you stopped at the end of a scene last time, and just can't get going this time, take the last page you've written, place it alongside your typewriter, and begin to retype it. By the time you've completed the retyping, you'll be in the swing of the script again and can go on from there.

And if that doesn't work, you'll have to do something drastic. It will tear your heart apart to do it, but do it if it is absolutely necessary. Take the last page of that script, rip it into small pieces, and throw it away. Don't throw it in your wastebasket; throw it out your window or flush it down the drain—anywhere where you will no longer have the temptation to snatch it up again and glue it together.

Then begin to write that page all over again. Don't try to write it word for word the same as the last time; write it as though you're doing something entirely new. You'd already thought this page out when you wrote it the last time, however, and as you work now, its phrasing and handling will come easily. You'll usually be able to finish it and keep going without pausing at the point where you stopped last time.

Big brother to the miniature work stoppage is the slump, the complete inability to work, which is supposed to strike most writers at least once in a lifetime, and which may last for months. Slumps are a favorite topic of conversation among writers, and I know a great many who have had them and suffered greatly while in the throes. You, however, can avoid them entirely by considering them squarely and recognizing them for what they are: the familiar subconscious why-I-should-stay-away-from-the-typewriter impulse, as described earlier in this chapter, enormously magnified by the writer's imagination.

A slump may be compared, in a way, to the paralyzed arm of a mental patient who has convinced himself so thoroughly that his arm is paralyzed that he will not feel a red-hot object pressed against it. You get dramatic proof of the lack of real paralysis, however, as I once did in the company of a client who writes medical material, when you watch the patient gravely wave his paralyzed arm up and down to show you how freely it used to move before the paralysis set in. There's an old joke to this effect, probably based on this sort of actual occurrence, which has been observed many times by psychiatrists.

The slump is every bit as real to the writer, who suffers agonies trying to snap out of it. He tries over and over again to write, but he's licked before he starts; he just knows he's in a slump and can't write, so of course he can't. Eventually his mind will succeed in casting off the idiot notion that his writing ability has miraculously vanished, and he is all right again; but there's no necessity to wait that long, or to allow the slump to start at all.

At least fifty times over the years, clients have come to my office and told me they're in a serious slump, and asked if I would advance them some money to pay their bills until they snap out of it. My answer has usually been the same: I tell them they've talked themselves into their slump, and that they can have the money if they will go into a vacant office in our suite and begin a script whose sale when completed will cover the amount advanced to them. Then I accompany them while they go into the office, and watch them pace back and forth for a while, and sit down in the chair and leap up again a few times, and finally begin painfully to write, groaning that the stuff is terrible and incoherent, as it has been every time they've tried lately. Of course, it isn't; it's a little rusty, perhaps, but generally in line with the quality of their output during normal periods. I push them some more, and they keep working; and after a while they're typing away rapidly, and the slump is over. I usually give them one final lecture before they leave with our check to pay their past-due bills, to make sure they don't go home and start convincing themselves all over again that they're in a slump.

Remember one thing, if you feel a slump coming on: writing ability isn't a shallow pan of water. It doesn't evaporate suddenly, and it doesn't dry out or get used up. (Investigate the few cases of writers who've "written themselves out" and vanished from the bookstores, and you'll find that each one vanished because he refused or unwittingly failed to adjust himself to new trends, or because he simply talked himself into believing that he was written out—a condition related to the slump. He will be back once the illusion fades.) If you force yourself to write and, most important, to complete scripts, however awful they may seem to you at the time, your slump will go just as it came.

One more psychological hurdle you'll want to leap is first-draftitis, the habit of writing loosely and carelessly because you know you can fix everything up in subsequent drafts. This one is a progressive disease: you'll find yourself writing more and more loosely and carelessly all the time, until your first drafts resemble nothing normal and require two dozen additional drafts to be made to read like professional scripts.

It's dangerous stuff, and it's even more dangerous if you use a word-processor because you know that you don't even have to face the manual labor of retyping after you've corrected your sloppy pages. You know that all you have to do is backspace to eliminate words and replace them with other words, and you know that you can stick words right into the middle of sentences, and shift sentences and paragraphs around and all the rest, and it's even fun doing it. But you'd better beware if you find yourself falling into the habit of using approximate words or phrases or sentences or paragraphs because you feel that you can fix them up when you go over the script. Before you know it, you'll discover that you can't come up with the right words or phrases or sentences or paragraphs when you want them. What you have done is blunt your naturally sharp word sense and feeling for language by too lax acceptance of substitutes when you should have been insisting on the originals.

The way to safeguard against this error is to write each page of your first draft as tightly and carefully as if it had to be sent to the editor the moment it was pulled out of the typewriter. It may slow you up a bit at first, but the net result—the habit of careful, tight writing—will be well worth it.

A great many writers ensure this by actually making the first draft their final draft: by typing right on white paper and sending their material to editors exactly as written. You may be unwilling to go to this extreme, and there's really no harm in allowing yourself a second draft in which you retype or use your word processor to make minor corrections.

But stop dead and get it straight the first time if you ever catch yourself thinking that, well, something isn't right but you can always fix it in the next draft.

6

YOUR ATTRACTIVE MERCHANDISE
The Professional-Looking Manuscript

The average editor's second home is his ophthalmologist's office. He goes there all too often for the treatment of eyestrain and related ailments, the result of the fact that every facet of his work—manuscript reading, proofreading of galleys, okaying of cover designs, reading of correspondence, writing of jacket copy, etc.—requires constant and steady use of his eyes. Not all editorial offices are the way they look in the movies, either, and sometimes the lighting in his sanctum sanctorum is very poor.

You can understand, therefore, why he will be unhappy if you send him a sloppy manuscript that is hard to read and that makes his aching eyes ache all the more. He may be the fairest-minded man in the world, but he will still find himself putting your script back at the bottom of the reading pile the first three or four times he comes to it, and then, when he does finally read it, he'll give it a far more cursory, fate-already-sealed examination than the other manuscripts in the pile. Several editors have stated publicly that the content is the thing, and that they would buy a good script if it came in written with a thick crayon on wrapping paper; but try and get them to name just one manuscript written on wrapping paper that they've actually bought in the past decade.

Most professionals realize this. They know that, though of course the writing and handling are the important things, there is a sort of psychological advantage in a beautifully prepared manuscript, and that a good novel in sloppy manuscript form somehow seems less good—and they go out of their way to make sure that their scripts are as professional in appearance as in content. So stop tapping your foot impatiently and thinking that manuscript preparation is minor stuff: nothing that may mean the difference between a prejudiced and an unprejudiced reading is minor.

On pages 44–46, I have included samples of the way the title page, the first pages of chapters, and the other pages of your manuscript should look. Use them as a guide, and keep the following important facts in mind:

1. Don't send handwritten manuscripts to editors. Type your manuscripts, or get someone to retype for you, if you handwrite your stuff. Some editors won't read handwritten material at all; none will read handwritten material as happily as typewritten material. Some small publishing houses, as a matter of fact, can't buy handwritten scripts even if they want to do so; they have no facilities for retyping the stuff or getting it retyped and they can't send handwritten scripts to the printers. (Many printers' contracts contain a clause stating that they will not set from handwritten copy.) And if you do your typing on a computer, make sure you have a letter-quality printer and not dot-matrix. I've seen editors turn into potential killers when they strain to read a dot-matrix manuscript.

2. Use a good grade of bond paper containing at least 25 percent rag or cotton, rather than sulfite paper, so that you can make erasures without blurring your words or rubbing holes in your manuscripts. The difference in price between rag and sulfite papers is moderate, and worth it. Don't, however, swing too far in the other direction and use one of those ultracrinkly kinds of paper that cost about a dime a sheet and look as though the government uses them to make currency. Pros who write regularly don't waste money on this kind of stuff, and it will mark you as a beginner.

3. Use standard 8 1/2" × 11" paper, and not legal or some other unusual size that won't fit in the editor's in-basket, desk drawer, or briefcase. Sixteen-pound is best; twenty-pound costs

```
                                                75,000 Words




                            THE DARKENED ROOM

                              A Novel by

                             Laura Maxwell




    Sally C. Carruthers
    105 Central Avenue
    Montrose, New York 10830
```

Figure 1. SAMPLE TITLE PAGE

THE DARKENED ROOM -- 305

THE VISITOR -- Chapter 16

Norcross stood there in the darkness for a moment, afraid to move and too nervous to stand still. Then, as the sounds in the hallway increased, he got down on his knees in the darkness and began to crawl forward, slowly, soundlessly.

He was halfway across the corridor when lights suddenly flared, and a beefy hand gripped the back of his neck. He knew from the enormous strength of the hand that it could belong to no one but Joseph J. O'Hara.

O'Hara's voice confirmed it. "Norcross! It isn't possible!"

Norcross got to his feet, and squirmed out of O'Hara's grasp to face him. He grinned feebly.

"Yes, it is, Mr. O'Hara," he said. "I was just going though."

"You're not going anywhere," O'Hara said. "What are you doing in my apartment, you miserable little flat-faced moron?"

"I was just going, Mr. O'Hara..."

"I want an answer to my question, you ugly twit," O'Hara said. "Did my wife let you into the apartment?"

"No, sir," Norcross said.

Figure 2. SAMPLE CHAPTER OPENER

THE DARKENED ROOM -- 306

"Then did the maid let you in? Did my son let you in? Did my daughter let you in?"

"No, sir. None of them seem to be here, sir."

"Then may I ask," O'Hara said gently, "how you got into my apartment?"

Norcross wiped a bead of sweat off his upper lip. "I climbed in through your living room window," he said. "It was open."

O'Hara's mouth was open, too. It hung that way for a while as he stared at Norcross.

"You should be careful about those things, Mr. O'Hara," Norcross went on, eagerly. "There are burglars in this town. Leaving windows open is a dangerous thing to..."

"Shut your mouth!" O'Hara said loudly. Then his voice quieted again. "Did you know you can get ten years for entering my apartment through a window that way, Norcross?" he asked. "Did you know I can call/cop and have you put away for ten long years?"

"Mr. O'Hara! You wouldn't!"

A dangerous grin lit up O'Hara's face. "No," he said. "I'm going to take you by your big nose and

Figure 3. SAMPLE PAGE OF TEXT

too much in the mails, and a lighter-weight paper creases and tears too easily.

4. Get the gum and goo out of your keys before you type the copy you're going to send to the editor. A good stiff typewriter brush and some carbon tet will do it, and the editor won't have to tear his hair out trying to decide whether those shapeless little blobs are *a*'s, *e*'s, *o*'s, *s*'s, or *c*'s, and whether or not he ought to go up to your place and stuff your manuscript down your throat.

5. Double-space your sheet, and leave at least one inch of white space on all sides. If the editor buys your manuscript, he'll need room to make corrections and alterations, if any, and write instructions to the printer.

6. When you come to an inch or so from the bottom of the page, just stop and go on to the next page; don't write "more." That's all right in newspaper writing, where each paragraph contains less important facts than the previous one, and a story can end practically anywhere; but there's something wrong with your book if the editor can't tell there's more when he comes to the bottom of a page.

7. When you reach the end of your script, just stop, or go down five single spaces and type a few dashes or "The End." Don't write "30," which means the end only to people familiar with newspaper tradition, and don't, if you want the editor to take you seriously, write "Finis."

8. As shown, put your real name and address on the title page, so that the editor will know where and to whom to write if he's interested; if you're using a pseudonym, put it under the title and put your real name with the address on the title page. If you work through an agent, put your name on the title page, but leave out your address—make it in care of your agent's name and address. That will give the editor the go-ahead to negotiate with your agent if he wants to contract for your book.

9. Put the approximate word count on the title page, but leave off such beginners' favorites as "For Sale" or "Usual Rates." The editor is aware that your script is for sale and not for rent or just to be admired, and he has his business office to remind him not to pay unusual rates. If you have a special reason for wishing to reserve certain rights—for example, if you're a resident of the British Isles and have already sold British rights to your book, and you've given Canadian rights to the British publisher even though these rights normally go to the American publisher—mention this in an accompanying note or underneath the word count; otherwise, leave it out entirely. Don't list an arbitrary restriction, such as "First Upper Half of Eastern New York State Rights Only," without reason. (Save the negotiation of rights for contract time. If you have an agent, of course, you should let him worry about the rights. That's part of his job.)

10. The word count, incidentally, should be to the nearest hundred; it need not be something like "74,673," which necessitates counting every word. You get the word count by counting several typical pages, arriving at an average amount of words per page, and multiplying it by the number of pages in the script. The count is more reliable, of course, when your typing is relatively uniform for each page, and many writers ensure uniformity by setting their typewriters and marking the paper so that they get an equal number of lines on all but the first and last pages of each chapter. If you use a word-processor, it will, of course, automatically print the same number of lines on each page before moving on to the next page.

11. A cover page at the back and front of the manuscript isn't a bad idea, since it will help keep the script clean through a good many submissions. Don't decorate it in any way, however; your name and address and the title are sufficient. If you work through an agent, skip the cover pages; he puts your script in a heavy cardboard box which protects it.

12. Up until a few years ago, it wasn't possible to copyright a totally unpublished work because publication and distribution were part of the copyright process, so a nervous author who wanted to copyright a script he hadn't been able to sell to a publisher had to go through a lot of elaborate nonsense including paying for and printing up some copies of his script and more or less placing those copies on sale with various people. It's a lot easier these days because changes in the copyright laws now allow the copyrighting of unpublished works: all you have to do is write to the Copyright Office, Library of Congress, Washington, D.C. 20559, for the forms necessary to copyright an unpublished work, fill out the simple forms when you receive them and send them to the Library of Congress together with a copy of your script and a check for $10.00, and the Copyright Office will copyright your script for you. Having told you all that, however, let me go on to say emphatically that, unless you're the type of consummate worrier who goes on worrying even in situations where knowledgeable people assure you there's nothing to worry about, you should *not* copyright your script. There is literally no piracy whatever in the American publishing business these days, and besides, under law, the very fact of your authorship gives you an automatic or common-law copyright. The publisher will copyright the book for you in your name, as a matter of routine, at publication time, and to secure copyright beforehand and list it is the sure sign of the amateur.

13. Don't fasten the pages or chapters of your script in any way; leave the pages loose. Editors like to flip through the pages easily and freely as they read. Paper fasteners and staples are hard to get out and sometimes cut the fingers, evoking much lack of merriment.

14. Put the name of your book and the page number, as shown, on every page. Sometimes the editor will pick up several scripts and drop them all, scattering the pages all over the floor.

He'll be grateful if the pages are identified and he can piece the scripts together rapidly.

15. Either the pica or elite typeface is acceptable to editors, provided it is clean and provided it is orthodox. Don't use special or fancy typewriters such as those that type all in italics, or all in capitals, or in Old English; they distract the editor while he's trying to read your script, which is the one thing you don't want to do. For the same reason, the ribbon should be medium-inked and black, not heavily and smudgily inked and blue or green or brown with yellow polka dots.

16. In general, keep in mind the fact that the primary function and purpose of the physical arrangement and appearance of your manuscript is to permit the editor to read it as easily and with as little distraction as possible. Such things as artistic borders drawn around the text will distract the editor; therefore, they're not to be used. Guide yourself with the rule that the neatest and most businesslike manuscript is the best-looking manuscript.

17. Type only on one side of the paper.

18. Don't quote a price for your manuscript, either on the script or in an accompanying letter. The publisher will prefer to make an offer.

19. If you want to emphasize a word or sentence or bit of dialogue, underline it, and it will be set up in italics when published. *(This sentence is in italics.)* If you leave out a word while typing, strike a diagonal (/) in the space in which it belongs and type the word in the line above. A listing of proofreaders' marks can be found in almost any good dictionary, but use these only when the galleys of your material are sent to you for correction. If there are a number of errors on pages of your manuscript, retype the pages.

20. When you are quoting something like a letter or a newspaper clipping in a manuscript, don't distinguish it from the rest of the script by typing it in single space. Nothing at all

in your manuscript should ever be typed in single space. Just indent an additional five spaces to the right of your regular paragraph indentation, and start your letter there. The different margin arrangement will make it stand out.

21. Indent paragraphs from five to seven spaces. Leave one space between words (not two, as a great many new writers do, for no discernible reason) and two spaces between sentences.

22. Generally, more writers use portables than standard models of typewriters, probably because they can be carted along when the owners wish to get a little writing done on trips and vacations. Almost every firm, incidentally, puts out a writers' model that includes such things as ready-made exclamation points (so that you don't have to bother stopping and holding one finger on your space bar while you hit the apostrophe and period with another), accent marks, etc. These cost a little more than the regular models, but they're worth it.

23. Don't forget to enclose return postage with each submission—and make sure you've sent enough to get the script back to you if it's rejected. Or, if you prefer, enclose a small check to cover costs, made payable to the publishing company, if you want your script sent back by Federal Express or UPS or some similar service.

24. Keep a copy of every script you send to market. Scripts get lost, shortened through the loss of pages in the editorial offices, and, if the editor reads at home and has a dog or an ungovernable temper, chewed up. It's a major disaster, of course, to lose a script, or to make a deal on a copyless script and have the publisher lose page 314 and wire you to rush your copy of the page at once.

25. And, finally, make sure that you have a fresh ribbon in your typewriter or computer printer when you're preparing your final copy, so that your machine will do more than make faint indentations in the paper. Remember the editor's sore eyes?

PART TWO

THE PLANNING AND PLOTTING FACTS

7

WHERE DO YOU GET YOUR IDEAS?
Tapping the Reservoir

Through the years, a number of mechanical devices have been placed on the market that offer to do your plotting and idea-getting for you. Generally, these work on a system whereby through the selection of cards or the use of a pointer or dial or where your computer selects an arbitrary group of plot elements and strings them together into an alleged story, you come up with a hero, heroine, villain, problem, and so forth. You flip your pointer, or dial your dial, or activate your computer, or select your cards, and get something like this:

Hero is a *coal miner*. Heroine is a *movie usherette*. Villain is *mayor of the town*. Problem is (hero and heroine are) *lost in the desert*. Complication is a *flood*. Solution comes about through a *candy bar*.

Probably you can work up a middling-fair plot from this conglomeration, and certainly it will test and exercise your ingenuity to figure out how, if your characters' problem is that they are lost in a desert, you can bring a flood into the situation. You will also have to do some mental acrobatics to puzzle out how this battle with the elements is won through the use of a candy bar, or how to give the villain something to do in this story where the troubles clearly come from a Higher Authority. I suppose the villain will have to get the hero and heroine lost in the desert for nefarious reasons of his own, and arrange the flood by loosing some gigantic irrigation system.

These mechanical devices make amusing games, but the fact must be faced that they really are little more than amusing games. They fail as legitimate suppliers of plots and ideas because there is no guarantee that the concoctions they serve up will make *your* kind of plot.

Don't misunderstand me: I don't mean that you'll be served a detective novel when your preference happens to be novels based on family problems. Most plotting devices offer different kinds of cards or gadgets or disks for different kinds of scripts. The example given, for instance, is a legitimate one that I worked out before beginning this chapter from a group of cards devoted to adventure novels. The series I used is a simplified one: some of the others give heroes' motives, villains' motives, further complications, and much more.

What I mean is that within the enormous areas of the general type of book you want to write (humorous mystery novel, war novel, historical novel, etc.), there are further considerations that can be determined only by your own particular personality and mental makeup. Perhaps vast and panoramic problems such as floods don't reach your emotions at all; perhaps you are emotionally moved by inner, more basic, problems, such as a man's fears that his wife has stopped loving him because he has taken her away from comfort to the life of a struggling and poverty-stricken farm, or a woman's fears at forty when she sees that romance has passed her by. Perhaps you know nothing about miners, or construction engineers, or television repairmen, or the other heroes selected by the plotting devices; perhaps you're interested in the troubles of young farmhands, or the worries of the sweet and lonely girl who works in the store down the street. The best scripts you will ever write are those that you understand and feel—books about the kinds of problems that move *you* emotionally just as you hope to move the reader emotionally—and it's an empty hope to expect to achieve exactly the right combination of events and people through the blind, close-your-eyes-and-stick-a-pin approach of mechanical plot devices.

Throughout my experience in the writing business, I have known only four authors who are successful and who used mechanical plot devices for any length of time. And when *they* discovered that by the time they had twisted and altered the plotting-device concoctions to fit their own emotional slant, their books bore no resemblance to the original schemes—that, in effect, they had been forming their scripts just as though they had not used the plotting devices at all—they discarded them. I apologize to the manufacturers of plotting devices for assaulting their product in this way, but it is my honest opinion that successful writing is too emotional and personal a thing to be built on so mechanical a framework.

The same basic flaw exists in all forms of homemade mechanical plotting as well: such as selecting six words at random from the dictionary and using them to build up an idea, or mentally selecting a page number and position in a news magazine and using the item that appears there, whatever it may be, as the basis for your next book. There is no assurance or promise that these things will fit *your* kind of emotions, or *your* way of thinking, and therefore they're useless to you.

The best way to get ideas for books is to draw on your personal experience. You'll need never worry about coming up with the wrong sort of idea, because your own mind and emotions will be doing the work for you. You may conjure up an idea that fits a field other than your specialty—a mystery-novel idea may turn up on rare occasions, when your usual field is family-problem novels—but it will always be an idea with which you are emotionally and personally *en rapport*. And, as you gain experience, your mind will school itself to think along the lines of your chosen field, just as it automatically and normally does along the lines of your emotional kind of script.

This personal plotting—this use of yourself as an idea well —never dries up or gets used up, because it is constantly replenished. It grows out of something to which you add every moment of your life: personal experience.

"Personal experience" is a sort of ambiguous phrase; it is interpreted by too many new writers to mean only the things that have happened to them personally. This is not the sole meaning at all: few of us live a lifetime's worth of book material.

Personal experience, in the idea-getting and book-planning sense, means anything at all that has come under your eye in any way at all. It means things that have happened to you, and things that have happened to your relatives and friends and acquaintances, and things about which you've heard in one way or another, and things you've learned in school, and things you've read about, or heard on the radio, or seen in the movies or on television. These things are part of your personal experience in the sense that you're aware of them.

If you know a man who is unhappy because his wife is so extravagant that she spends more money on her own clothing than on the upkeep of their children; if you hear about a man who is ruining his life because he can't break his gambling habit; if you read a story about a man who is miserable because he has been forced into a profession other than the one of his choice, you've added further material to your mental file. And nearly everybody runs across that sort of thing a dozen times a week.

This doesn't mean, when you're settling down to write a book, that it will necessarily be about a man whose wife is extravagant, or a man who gambles, or a man who is in the wrong profession. It is the basic causes *behind* these cases that are important to you—the basic factors that cause human troubles.

Your man-in-wrong-job novel need not be, for example, about an architect who wishes he were a doctor, if that were the situation in the story you read. The basic factor is maladjustment to circumstances, so your novel may be about a timid little bookkeeper who wishes he were an explorer—or, perhaps, an explorer who wishes he had some nice safe job like bookkeeping. The real-life case of the man who gambles may be very sad indeed: but if you write funny novels, and understand the case in its essential ingredient—the fact that people sometimes can't seem to stop themselves from doing things they know are wrong—you can work up an amusing script about a man who really loves his fiancée but is in trouble with her because he can't seem to break the habit of becoming involved with every pretty girl he meets.

Every human problem of which you are aware can be transmuted into a dozen different book ideas, or a hundred dozen. The extravagant-woman case can become a very serious novel about a man who loves his wife but is torn between two loves when he discovers that she hates their children (perhaps because they've cut down her personal freedom—or perhaps they're his children by a previous marriage); it can become a light-hearted script about a man who loves his wife but must cure her of some annoying habits or mannerisms, or go mad; it can become the study of a man who resents his wife's dedication to her own career and her neglect of the family, but eventually discovers that he has been selfish in other, more important, ways; it can become the story of a woman who is so concerned about her easygoing husband that she secretly creates crises in their life, so that he'll be forced by circumstances to be more aggressive and realistic; it can become the motive in a crime novel. And so on, ad infinitum.

This transmutation of everyday occurrences into book ideas, understand, will usually not be a deliberate or conscious process, particularly after you've been working at writing for a while. Few writers actually sit down and say to themselves, "Now, what actual occurrence would be suitable as a start-off point?" Most of the time, your ideas will come from springboards deeply embedded in your subconscious; you'd require the assistance of a team of psychoanalysts to help you trace them back to their initial sources. That is why I say that your storehouse is adding material all the time: with your mind working for you and clicking away every hour of the day, mechanical plotting remains an unnecessary and poor substitute.

You may, of course, have to draw on personal experience consciously at the start, and on those rare later occasions when your subconscious doesn't seem to be functioning right.

Some writers get ideas when they're working on other scripts and don't need them, or when they're doing things other than book planning or writing, and then have a devil of a time remembering them or forcing up others when they're ready to begin work on their next scripts. Other writers can usually sit down and work up a good idea any time they need one. If you're in the latter group, you require nothing but congratulations; if you're in the former, get yourself a good stiff-backed notebook and jot down ideas as they come to you. You can also stick into your notebook any clippings that suggest ideas to you.

Three important tips to notebook users. First, don't note down your ideas in such detail that you feel you've done the thing before you settle down to write the script, but don't make them too scanty, either. One of my clients once wrote, "Guy needs heebles," in his notebook; he's sure it was a first-class idea, but he's been trying for years to remember what it was. Second, don't keep ideas in your notebook too long without using them: ideas have a way of refreshing themselves over and over again while they're in the back of your mind, but they grow cold and useless when they remain too long in your notebook. And third, don't discuss your ideas. You'll find they'll have lost their excitement or flavor when you get down to the actual writing.

Most writers get their ideas and work out a mental plan of the script before they begin writing; a very few sometimes begin writing without an idea at all, and try to develop a plot by leading off with a character in trouble or in some unusual situation. The writing-without-a-compass method sometimes works, because the mind swings into action and manages to come forth with a stored-up idea that fits the opening situation, but generally it's bad medicine. You can stack up quite a pile of disjointed and *unfinished* scripts that way.

Most of the time, you definitely need a good idea and a plan of action before you begin writing. In the chapters that follow, we're going to discuss the method of building your ideas into salable plots, and take a look at exactly how much pre-writing planning is needed.

8

PLOTS THAT SELL
How to Build Your Ideas into Salable Books

Let's talk about skeletons. One particular skeleton, as a matter of fact: an important little item known as the plot skeleton.

The plot skeleton is my name for it, anyway. Other people have called it the general plot pattern, the universal plot, the basic plot structure, the interior fiction framework, and a few dozen other things. Whatever name you give it, it is something that will be completely useless to you if you don't fully understand it—and your best friend in the writing business if you do.

The plot skeleton is the basic structure underlying almost every piece of commercial fiction from fairy tales to classics *to best-sellers* to the stories in the magazine on the corner newsstand. This common denominator runs along these lines:

A sympathetic lead character finds himself in trouble of some kind and makes active efforts to get himself out of it. Each effort, however, merely gets him deeper into his trouble, and each new obstacle in his path is larger than the last. Finally, when things look blackest and it seems certain that the lead character is *finished,* he manages to get out of his trouble through his own efforts, intelligence, or ingenuity.

Now let's make a simple test. Can you think of lots of books that are not built around the plot skeleton as described? Do you believe that only a small portion of published novels *are* built around the plot skeleton as described? That's our test—for if you have answered yes, you have indicated that you don't really understand the plot skeleton as you should.

What you're forgetting, as so many people do, is that the plot skeleton *is* a skeleton—and that it may look so different with one layer of outer flesh than with another that it's hard to believe the two are identical inside. Remember that when you take two female skeletons and cover them differently, one is an ordinary woman and the other is Sophia Loren. They are still, however, identical in skeletal structure.

The plot skeleton in its simplest or most obvious form—the form many inexperienced writers assume, very wrongly, all plot skeleton scripts must take—is the one in which the lead character gets into trouble that is big, surface, and physical: let us say, by way of example, that he is framed for a murder. He makes an active physical effort to get out of trouble—let us say he sneaks up into the murder room to examine the evidence and sees if he can find some clue to the real killer—and the way this deepens his trouble is also surface and obvious to all who read the book: the cops enter the room suddenly and, though he manages to elude them and escape, they're surer than ever that he's guilty because they assume he came up there to destroy the evidence against him.

Then he makes another physical effort to get out of his trouble—he sneaks over to see the chief witness in the hope that he can get the truth out of her—and again the further deepening of his trouble is obvious: he's a little rough about it in his eagerness, and she believes (or pretends to believe) that he's trying to kill her; she screams and he runs away, and, when the police come, she says he's certainly the murderer because he just tried to kill her to shut her up. Some more physical efforts to clear himself—some more unintended results which make him look guiltier than ever—and then, when things look blackest and he's just about to enter prison for life, he works out something through his own intelligence, efforts, or ingenuity that enables him to trap or unmask the real murderer and clear himself.

You don't need a strong magnifying glass to see the plot skeleton in that novel; its bones stick out along the surface every inch of the way. You can take a pencil and encircle each ingredient as it turns up in the story: the trouble—the efforts to overcome the trouble—the deepening of the trouble with each effort—the reaching of the peak point of despair—followed by the solution through the lead character's own efforts. The book is a perfectly salable example of the basic plot skeleton structure in fiction, but it is not the only one.

Let's have a look at another example: a romantic novel wherein the man and woman fall in love and then become estranged due to a series of misunderstandings in which each partner arrives at false conclusions about the other's character. They still love each other, basically, and the man makes a number of efforts to win the lady back—but, sadly enough, estranges her further with each effort. And then, finally, he manages to succeed in winning her back, and they live, let us hope, happily ever after.

Here the plot skeleton is a little deeper below the surface, but it is still not hidden too much. The trouble is not physical danger, as in the previous example, but it is still trouble: the hero may lose forever the woman he loves. He makes definite efforts to overcome his trouble and win her back, and just as definitely moves the goal farther away than ever in doing so. And finally, when things are blackest and it seems certain that the romance will never resume, the hero succeeds in overcoming his trouble and winning the lady back. A number of people, however, will solemnly list this novel as an example of one that does not contain the plot skeleton structure.

Let's take one more novel: one about a man who has grown rather used to his wife and his comfortable home life and fancies himself in love with a slick young chick who works in his office and who represents to him a more exciting way of living. He manages to anesthetize his conscience a little and rationalize his actions—despite an inner gnawing feeling of guilt—by blaming the marital breakup on his wife's coldness and by thinking that a freer kind of life is just what he's been missing for so long. But at the end, for any one of a variety of reasons, he has come to know that his wife is best for him, and he goes back to her.

There may be little physical action in this script: it may even be, throughout, a story of a struggle in a man's mind. When it is well done, the plot skeleton is not visible to the inexpert or semiexpert eye at all, but it is built on a plot skeleton structure just as definitely as the other examples. It is a plot skeleton in every way: there is trouble—the man's indecision between his wife and the young girl; his efforts to solve it are his mental churning and the battle between his rationalization and the feeling of guilt; it grows blacker because his mental struggles and strife make him less and less able to decide which choice is the right one; and the trouble is overcome when he makes the right choice and goes back to his wife.

You've taken five giant steps in the direction of intelligent planning when you understand that the plot skeleton is not just a formula for one kind of novel—that it is not a formula at all —but rather a listing of the basic ingredients that go into the making of nearly all fiction of all types. A fiction formula is a restricting affair that shows you how to do a specific kind of script in a specific way; the plot skeleton names the basic ingredients and then allows you to mold and use them in any way you see fit. To assume that plots must be routine or along a single trail because they contain specific basic ingredients is to assume that all cakes must be alike because they all contain flour and sugar, or that all books must be the same because they're all made up of words and punctuation marks.

You'll find it impossible, I think, to detect external resemblances between the crime novel described in this chapter and that great character study and modern classic *Goodbye, Mister Chips*—yet both contain the same internal structure. Analyze the Hilton novel and you'll see that it is about a man with a problem (the fear that he'll fail at the work that means his entire life to him—teaching), who makes active efforts to overcome the problem (by being hard and stern because he believes these are the qualities most required in a good teacher), but whose continued efforts only make the problem blacker (he fails more and more as a teacher because the students hate him for his sternness), and who finally solves his problem by becoming, through the example of his sweet and gentle wife, kind and understanding to his students—and thereby a great and beloved teacher.

Nor, among the infinite variety of novels built around the plot skeleton, must the lead character always be aware of his problem at the start, or always solve it happily. Sydney Carton, in *A Tale of Two Cities,* for example, resolves the problem of his weakness of character by doing "a far, far better thing" than he has ever done before—he gives his life for the happiness and safety of others. In some plots, as a matter of fact, the solution need not even be certain: the book may end on the note that there is hope for happiness at last, or that it looks as though everything is going to be all right.

One other variation is the inverted plot skeleton, the exact opposite of the standard plot skeleton. In the regular plot skeleton script, attention is focused on a sympathetic lead character, and reader interest is built up through the fear that he may not succeed in solving his problem—until, at the end, he does. In the inverted skeleton novel, of which one famous example is Forsyth's *The Day of the Jackal,* the lead character is a villain who succeeds more and more in his evil doings, and reader interest is held through the fear that he'll succeed completely —until, at the end, he fails.

The best way to understand the reason for the plot skeleton is to examine its makeup.

The reason for the need of a definitely sympathetic or unsympathetic lead character is a simple one: if your reader doesn't care much about your lead—if he neither likes nor dislikes him particularly—he isn't going to be much interested in what happens to him. You've got to make absolutely sure that your reader is cheering or jeering your lead if you want him to remain interested all the way through.

You can see the reason for the basic problem, of course: a smooth-running life is pleasant to watch, but it doesn't grip a reader's interest for long. The moment a character he likes gets into trouble, however, it's another thing again—he's right alongside, rooting for him all the way. And that, too, is the reason for the complications—the constant sinking deeper and deeper into the pit, the constantly larger and larger rocks in the path to safety. If a problem looks easy to solve, why worry about it?

And when things have reached their lowest ebb, when the black clouds are thickest, and the hero finally manages to solve his problem—he's got to do it himself. As you can understand, it's pretty frustrating to watch an admirable character struggle and struggle against obstacles; and then, at the end, see somebody else get him out of the jam. You're more than a little disappointed in the man, and you also feel cheated. Keep the fortuitous arrival of the U.S. Marines out of your scripts; if your character's worthy of being the lead in your novel, he should be strong enough to do all the final problem-solving personally. There have been some pretty fair books in which someone other than the lead solves the problem at the end, but they would have been infinitely more satisfying if the lead had done the job himself.

When you've got a good idea for a book—which is usually just another way of saying that you've worked up a strong and fresh problem and a strong and fresh solution—use the plot skeleton to work out the details, and then use it as a yardstick to see that everything is O.K. If all the bones are strong, and all the bones are there, you won't ever have to worry about having a sick plot.

9

WHEN IS A NOVEL NOT A NOVEL?
Incident Versus Novel

Let's see if we can work up a quick freehand definition of a novel on the basis of the discussion of plotting in the preceding chapter. It would probably run something like this:

A novel is a description of events stemming from a problem and eventually resulting in resolution of that problem. To put it another way, it is what happens when someone has a problem and overcomes it.

I've stated it simply and basically because I want you to note one particular thing: a novel follows a straight and well-defined line from beginning to end. In a nutshell, it moves from the basic problem (whether it is a struggle against visible trouble or a man's strife within his own mind or whatever) directly to the resolution of that problem (whether it is happy or unhappy or definite or just hopeful for the future or what have you). There are boulders in the path—the difficulties in solving the problem, which build up suspense and nail the reader to his chair—but it is a straight path leading to a definite and desired-by-the-reader destination.

That is a novel. Now let's see if we can work up a definition of an incident:

An incident is a description of an event or series of events, and nothing more. It does not necessarily go anywhere or make any definite point.

The difference between the two, in other words, is that the first describes events with a definite reason for doing so—the events are moving the novel toward the solution of a conundrum established at the beginning; the other describes an event or events for the mere sake of describing them.

The presence of urgency-to-reach-a-particular-destination in a novel and its absence in an incident is the reason for the fact that a novel is salable and an incident is not. A novel holds the reader's interest and keeps him interested throughout; an incident merely tells him about something in which there's no reason or necessity for him to be interested at all.

A great many new writers, for example, believe they are writing a salable novel when they tell the tale of a boy and girl who meet in an office and like each other and decide to get married. This isn't a novel at all; it is something you tell in a letter to someone who knows the boy and girl and therefore has a personal reason for being interested. It is of no interest to the reader of fiction because it follows a routine course and contains nothing to worry him and grip his attention. Even if they meet in an unusual way and fall in love in an unusual way and the marriage ceremony is performed while they're standing on their heads on a plane wing, nothing more is achieved than a casual and fleeting interest at each unusual occurrence—because the novel lacks the *sustained* attention that comes with never-lessening worry over a strong problem and whether or not it can be overcome.

You have a novel when the boy and girl break up for some reason—when a basic problem arises—and then their efforts to get together just drive them farther apart (the complications) —and when it finally looks as though they'll never get together (the things-look-darkest point)—and when they finally *do* get together. The reader can sigh with relief at *this* conclusion because he has had his vicarious thrill of worrying over whether or not they would get together at all. Naturally, he sort of knew that they would get together at the end, but the increasing blackness of the storm clouds gave him a you-never-can-tell feeling that is completely lacking in the untroubled and foregone-conclusion incident.

The incident, for that matter, could even have ended with the characters deciding not to get married after all, and the reader wouldn't have cared particularly. It's just too late when you wait until the end of a novel to remember that a reader must worry to enjoy. You've given him no reason to worry that things may go wrong—all you've done is told the dull and placid story of a dull and placid courtship—so what the devil is it to him if you decide at the end to have the boy and girl split up?

The vital factor, in fiction, of a problem and the hard fight to overcome it and its eventual overcoming has been given a great many technical names. The one that describes the necessity of moving steadily toward a definite destination is frequently called story-line delineation; the one that describes the struggles in overcoming the problem is frequently called conflict. Whatever the names, however, you just can't do without it.

The conflict may be outward—as in a struggle of man against man, or man against circumstances or events; and it may be inward—as in a man's mental struggle against himself; but it must be there. A novel without struggle is no novel at all.

Undoubtedly, many writers turn out incidents because they're unaware of these facts and believe they are writing novels; others do so deliberately because they've seen some very fine novels published that they believe are only incidents. These writers would do well to look again. A novel like the one about the man who's too used to his wife and falls for a young girl but at the end decides to return to his wife, for example, might easily appear to be an incident, particularly when there's relatively little external action. It is not an incident, however; it is a complete and satisfying story because it contains all the necessary elements of the problem and the struggle to overcome it and its final overcoming.

You'll find this to be true as well of almost all other published novels that may at first appear to be nothing more than incidents. The characters may even do nothing but sit around and talk from the first line to the last, but there is definite *direction* in the things they are saying—a special undertone in the conversation that moves inevitably toward the resolution of the basic problem. Even ultraliterary novels move from a basic problem to an ultimate resolution of the problem: though here, in the field where sorrow so often reigns supreme, the resolution is often that You Can't Win and the character had better learn to suffer in silence.

An incident, you must also keep in mind, can only be made into a novel by the addition of a basic problem and movement toward solution; never simply by the addition of more incidents, as some people suppose. This illusion probably arises from unawareness of the difference between the dictionary definition of the word and its meaning in fiction writing.

The dictionary defines an incident as a single event or happening; the fiction field defines it as an isolated or self-contained occurrence of any kind—in the sense that it is just "a piece" and not a full story line. The typical incident example —boy and girl meet and like each other and decide to get married—would, for instance, be only a small part of an acceptable novel or story: probably just the occurrence before they break up and the problem starts.

To put it another way, a script doesn't avoid being an incident merely because it covers a number of scenes rather than just one: if the whole thing sums up as a problemless and conflictless occurrence, it is an unsalable incident, even if it takes a hundred scenes to tell. Boy-and-girl-meet-and-like-each-other-and-decide-to-get-married misses because it lacks suspense and the factors that grip and hold a reader's attention; it doesn't become any more suspenseful and reader-gripping if the boy and girl meet and begin to like each other in Scene One, meet at the same place the next day and like each other some more in Scene Two, go to a disco together and like each other some more in Scene Three, decide to become engaged in Scene Four, get together and arrange for the wedding in Scene Five, and so on and so on and so on and so on and so on.

It doesn't even help if they have a little tiff in Scene Six and make up in Scene Seven, and another little tiff and reunion in

Scenes Eleven and Twelve, because these are little pebbles that hardly mar the walk up Lovers' Lane. You get your reader and hold him only by bringing your problem onstage early and making it darker and darker as you go along. That basic problem is a big boulder blocking the road, the subsequent complications make it even bigger, and when the problem reaches its crisis—when things look blackest—it's a mile high. A few scattered pebbles just aren't in the same league.

Some more huzzahs for the plot skeleton, in conclusion, because you'll always write a complete novel if you follow it carefully. We'll put each of its bones under a microscope in the next few chapters.

10

THE BIG HEADACHE
The Problem

Two simple words are your best yardsticks for measuring the strength of your story problems. Mark them down: *must* and *cannot.*

The lack of one or the other of these, or both of them, is the chief reason for the rejection of so many scripts on the grounds of weakness of the basic problems. It is the chief reason that so many scripts are rejected as "too slight," for editors usually use this phrase to cover any script in which the basic problem and its resulting events just don't seem adequate to retain the reader's interest.

Some examples will illustrate this.

Let's say that you have a character named Jimmy Jones, who wakes up one morning and decides that he's finally going to buy a house and move his family out of the cramped apartment in which they've lived for years. He leaps into his trousers and washes and shaves and finishes dressing and breakfasts hurriedly, and the rest of the script follows him as he looks at various unsuitable houses, and then finds a good one and buys it.

Strictly speaking, Jones has a problem: the finding and buying of a suitable house. For fiction purposes, however, it just isn't enough, for his problem lacks the *must* ingredient—an urgency or pressing necessity to find and buy the house. Since he won't be in trouble or any the worse off if he doesn't find and buy one, the reader has no strong reason to worry over or be interested in his search.

All right, you correct it. You have Jones awakened by a

phone call from an attorney, who tells him that Ebenezer Jones, his eccentric great-uncle, has just passed on. Under the terms of Ebenezer's will, young Jimmy will inherit a vast fortune (which will, incidentally, enable him to get Mrs. Jimmy the fantastically expensive operation required to save her life, which he cannot afford otherwise), provided he manages to own and live in a house that same night. Jimmy yanks out his savings—enough to buy a house, though not to pay for the surgery—and rushes off and buys one, thereby winning the vast fortune.

Now you're closer, for he has a definite and urgent reason that he *must* get that house—but you're still not there. However urgent a problem may be, it still isn't worrisome if it can be easily solved. And Jimmy's problem can, of course, because all he has to do is rush out and buy a house. The ingredient of *cannot* is lacking.

You get your genuinely strong and adequate problem if Ebenezer made his fortune by building green houses with red gables, and insists, for sentimental reasons, that the house his heir must own be a green one with red gables—and there just aren't any of that description close enough (even by plane) for Jimmy to reach and buy and live in, all by that night. You've got a problem with a must—Jimmy *must* find that house because he needs the vast fortune to save his wife's life—and it seems that he *cannot* find it, because there aren't any of that sort around. If Jimmy is a sympathetic and likeable lead character, you'll have little trouble keeping your reader around to watch him fight to solve this worrisome problem.

Of course, I've poked a little fun at trite plotting with this example—odd wills and wives who need operations immediately have been done to death—but I think the point is clear. If your problem lacks urgency, or if it can be easily solved, it isn't doing properly or fully the job for which it has been set up: to worry the reader over its outcome.

You must never make the mistake of assuming that your reader will automatically be interested in your book. You've got to remember that your reader is a human being with troubles and concerns of his own, and his attention will lag if you don't pull him quickly out of his own world into the world of your script. You do it best when you give him the kind of problem that could conceivably confront *him*, because that establishes reader identification, but it must be a problem so interestingly urgent and apparently insoluble that it defeats his natural tendency to give his attention to his own concerns.

This does not mean, obviously, that every problem you choose in writing your books must be a life-or-death affair; it means that within the limits of the kind of script you're writing, you've got to make the problem so logically worrisome to the lead character that the reader will begin to worry along in sympathy. In the light romantic novel, for example, the reader doesn't expect or require dire circumstances or disaster, but the hero's desire to get the girl must still be made urgent and important enough—despite the lighthearted circumstances that keep them apart—that the reader will remain continually interested in their efforts to get together.

It's those two all-important ingredients at work again: must and cannot. For despite the relative unimportance of the boy-wants-girl-he's-recently-met problem compared to, let us say, one involving a man's struggle to save his life, the successful light love story becomes important by convincing the reader that the boy *must* have that girl and, for one reason or another, it seems that he *cannot*.

Another thing you must remember is that urgency of problem means immediacy as well as importance to the lead character. As a result, an important-to-the-hero and apparently unsoluble problem will nevertheless be inadequate if it is something that occurs again and again and has no special reason for immediate solution as your book opens. An example might be a farmer's year-after-year battle against locusts. This problem may certainly be important to him to solve, because it's ruining his farm, and it may be apparently insoluble because he just can't seem to get rid of the pests, but it lacks adequate urgency because he has been fighting the locusts for years and may be doing so for years longer. It would become an urgent problem only if the locusts are arriving for the first time, and he has to get rid of them at once or watch his crop ruined in a matter of hours or days; or, if they've been coming for years and his farm is almost barren and, as the book opens, they're coming again and he has to get rid of them at once *this* time or be ruined completely. In both cases, of course, to complete the urgency, he'd make strong but unsuccessful efforts to get rid of them—and manage it only when things look blackest.

Generally, job and money problems fall into the same category: they usually aren't adequate by themselves. If the lead is struggling to get money—let's say a particular sum of money, such as a cash first prize in a contest—just for the sake of getting money, it isn't sufficient because there's no real urgency or pressing necessity for that money, and no real trouble if he doesn't get it. If the lead is struggling to keep his job just for the sake of keeping his job, it fails because the reader's casual reaction is that he can always get another job if he loses this one. There must, therefore, be a special and urgent need for that money—anything but the old wife-needs-an-expensive-operation-immediately, please—or a particular and urgent reason that he must keep the job.

Sometimes, a problem with inadequate urgency can be made adequately urgent if it is tied in with a psychological characteristic of your lead, or some other psychological factor. The problem of a man who may lose his job and who is struggling to keep it just for the sake of keeping it is not, as I have said, usually an adequate one, but it becomes adequate if, for example, the lead character has lost a number of jobs in the recent past and will lose the last fragments of his self-confidence and self-respect if he is dropped from *this* job. If well done, the problem has actually been altered from the weak one of a man struggling to keep his job to the strong one of a man struggling to retain his mental balance.

Another example might be the story of a boy who wants a

dog but is opposed by the adults with whom he lives. Hundreds of new writers turn out very fresh variations on this theme but find their scripts are rejected because the problem isn't strong enough. (The boy really wouldn't be too much the worse off if he didn't get the dog.) The difference between these novels and a salable one is that the latter would add a psychological factor: the boy, for example, is an orphan living with cold and unaffectionate foster parents and, the reader realizes, he *must* have the dog to fill his psychological need for love and affection.

Almost any problem becomes strong enough with *must* and *cannot* ingredients added, through psychological angles or any other. Even our old pal Jimmy Jones could get by with hunting for his house just to get a house if the script would show believably and sympathetically that the hope for this house has been his one dream in life, and that, for some reason, he must get it now or never.

One of the most apt descriptive titles ever given an illness —in this case a story illness—is "paper dragon." Its name explains it: a paper dragon is a monster that looks real and fearsome at first, but that turns out, on closer examination, to be made only of paper.

The paper dragon script is one in which the lead character believes he has a serious problem and spends the entire book trying to overcome that problem, only to discover at the end that the problem never existed at all. A typical paper dragon might be one in which a woman decides that her husband doesn't love her anymore, goes through all sorts of emotional and mental travail in her efforts to correct the situation, and then discovers at the end that he *does* love her after all—that the only reason he didn't get her a birthday present was that he had to save up one more day's subway fare to buy that sixty-thousand-dollar sable coat.

You don't need a crystal ball to imagine the average reader's reaction to that sort of thing. Here he has sweated along with the heroine all through the book under the assumption that she had a serious problem—here he was wasting all that sympathy—and it turns out that she had no problem at all, except perhaps her moronic tendency to jump to conclusions. Publishers, of course, spare readers this reaction by bouncing paper dragon scripts as rapidly as they spot them.

Let me state this in a throbbing, pleading voice: when you give your reader a strong problem to worry over, make sure it remains a strong problem, which the lead character manages to resolve at the end. Don't let it turn out to be one of those gee-I-was-wrong-I've-no-problem-after-all affairs, or I make no guarantee for your personal safety if one slips into print. It isn't a hard mistake to make, either, so watch it.

Blood relative to the paper dragon script is the "idiot plot," also called the "Hollywood plot," because of the movie colony's supposed partiality to it. It gets its name from the fact that the only thing that keeps the problem from being resolved almost at the start is that the characters act like idiots in order to keep the plot moving.

In the idiot plot script, for example, the hero, a doughnut salesman, misses a date with the heroine because his employer has sent him suddenly out of town to line up a big doughnut eater in Poughkeepsie. The heroine automatically assumes, for no discernible reason, that the hero was out with some girl, so she rushes off to her grandmother's home to be consoled. The hero, returning and rushing to see the girl to apologize and tell her of the big order he's snagged, finds her away and, without discernible reason, assumes she is away with some man, and goes off to *his* grandmother to be consoled. Later they meet and, proudly, tell each other that they had been out on dates those days. ("If she thinks that, the bitch, I'll let her think so!" "If he thinks that, the rat, I'll let him think so!")

By all the rules of logic, their spat would have been settled in three minutes if they had acted like normal human beings at any of the several opportunities presented and made the simple explanations necessary. Instead they act in just the opposite manner, the only possible reason being that if they did explain, the book would be over. In some idiot plot scripts, the characters' adroitness at doing the illogical thing is truly remarkable.

The *cannot* ingredient must be legitimate: the strong problem will hold up only if the lead character cannot solve it however hard he tries. If he misses solving the problem early in the game only because of his own stupidity, or by missing opportunities a man in his position would not logically miss, the answer is that you haven't a strong, apparently insoluble problem. He must be defeated in his efforts to solve the problem because *anybody* would be defeated.

One more problem pitfall is the "white elephant," wherein the lead character struggles through the first half of the novel to get something—and then discovers that he doesn't want it after all, and struggles through the second half to get rid of it. If a problem is worth struggling to solve at all, the solution must bring worthwhile and satisfactory results. The white elephant story also defeats its own purpose, because it reveals that if the thing the lead struggles to get turns out to be unneeded, there was no real urgency behind his struggles in the first place: he was just foolish in thinking there was.

And one last problem to avoid is the borrowed-trouble variety, which occurs in the hero-sticks-his-nose-in-somebody-else's-business novel. This is the one wherein, in its worst examples, the hero just barges into some situation that is no business of his at all, and bustles around for the rest of the book solving a problem in which he has no personal stake. (For example, a newspaper-reporter hero is sent to get the story on a body found in a hotel room, and spends the rest of the yarn running around acting like a cop and trying to solve the murder—ignoring his newspaper job so completely that he never even phones in details of developments.) In its slightly less terrible examples, it is the one in which the hero has some acquaintance who is in trouble and goes to work to get him out of it.

In any of its examples, this sort of book is not as satisfying, or anywhere nearly as salable, as the book in which the problem is the lead character's own, and he struggles to solve it because it is personally necessary that he do so. The reader's attention is held in fiction when he is made to feel sympathetic toward the lead character, and the reader is, therefore, interested in watching him solve the strong problem that confronts him. His interest will be greatly lessened, and often dissolved entirely, if the problem turns out to be someone else's altogether.

A novel may be acceptable if the lead character works to get his fiancée, or his wife, or his kid brother, or his best friend, out of a jam, because that really isn't borrowed trouble: if it is established that he loves the person very much, the person's troubles are almost his. Otherwise, the vogue for the I-do-it-because-I'm-interested-in-people novel has passed; perhaps we've all just become too cynical and self-centered. Anyway, ninety-nine out of a hundred borrowed-trouble scripts would be enormously improved if the helping-hand lead were heaved out entirely and the person in trouble became the lead, with the problem to overcome for himself.

11

HIT HIM WHEN HE'S DOWN
Complications

Hollywood is going to do a little work for us in this chapter. It's going to provide an example of a hero whose problem complications are so good that they aren't any good at all.

All this happens in a movie, of course: one in which the hero is a man who has been arrested and convicted for a murder he did not commit. Later, he is helped to escape from prison by the heroine, who feels sympathy toward him because her father had died in prison following conviction for a crime *he* did not commit. The hero returns to his old neighborhood to try to clear himself by finding the real murderer.

After several attempts, during which the police grow hotter and hotter on his trail, and things look blacker and blacker, he succeeds: he discovers and confronts the real murderer, an older woman. She admits it calmly, pointing out, however, that he can be cleared only if she is around to be made to confess publicly. And then, before he can stop her, she underlines her hatred for him by leaping out of a window to her death.

I remember feeling considerable admiration for the scriptwriters at this point. Here, I thought, was complication-upon-complication-to-reach-blackest-point-of-despair at its best. Now the hero *really* seemed to be sunk. I wondered how he was going to get out of it.

And then my admiration dissolved into little pieces, because he just didn't. He shrugged his shoulders in despair, and the final scene showed the hero and heroine meeting happily by arrangement in a South American country where extradition is not permitted.

The movie, in short, had settled for a plain, garden-variety insult to the intelligence. It expected the audience to believe that a man of the hero's strength of character and determination could live the rest of his life happily and contentedly away from the country of his birth, forever in exile for a crime he knew he had not committed.

What the writers had done was overshoot their mark. They had worked so hard to make the problem complications blacker and blacker, and apparently insoluble, that they had made it really insoluble. And so they had been forced to fall back on a solution that could not fail to dissatisfy, particularly in view of the fact that the rest of the picture had been devoted to the hero's gigantic efforts to clear himself. He could, after all, have gone to the South American country right after his escape. His problem was to clear himself, not to avoid recapture, and that problem remained unsolved at the picture's end.

The purpose of complications in your scripts, as we have discussed, is to increase and continue to increase the tension that you set up in the reader when you first show him the problem confronting the sympathetic lead character. Their purpose is also to increase his desire to see the problem solved and to frustrate the desire with each new and greater complication until you fulfill it at the end of the script. You must, therefore, make sure that the complications are sufficiently black to build up that worry and desire but not so black that you find yourself unable at the end to furnish the lead with the relief he deserves.

The killer's suicide in the picture was an error of technique because it did actually shut off the hero's last avenue of solution of his problem: it would have been perfectly acceptable if it had only *seemed* to shut off that last avenue, because it sank the hero and the audience in the necessary deepest depth of despair. If the hero had managed to solve his problem despite that final kick in the heart, the film would have been an entirely satisfactory one instead of a quite good one that fell apart at the end.

When you plan your problem and complications, it's usually safest to plan your solution at the same time. If you just go ahead and write your script up through the final complication, without knowing how you're going to end it, you're liable to find yourself just as puzzled about a logical solution as your lead character. And then, as in the movie just described, you may be strongly tempted to conclude with a weak device, and that isn't good. Your reader will never be satisfied if the neutron bomb you've built goes off with a bang as loud as a sheet of paper dropped on a thick rug.

Complications are like sunbaths: they miss their purpose if each new one doesn't make things a little darker.

Every complication faces the danger of being nothing more than an out-and-out irritant to the reader. All complications are irritants, in a way, because they keep the reader temporarily from seeing what he wants to see: the lead character solve the problem. Complications that rise out the lead's efforts to solve the problem, and that make the situation look blacker, have a definite purpose—the stronger the pain, the sweeter the relief—and you can get away with them because the hero is doing what the reader wants him to do (struggling to solve the problem) and the complications are logical, if unfortunate, results. But when a complication occurs "on the side"—when it does not result from the lead's direct efforts to solve his problem —it accomplishes nothing more than to delay the story movement and cut its suspense; it irritates the reader without any compensating factors whatever.

Take, for example, the familiar complication that occurs when the lead character is speeding along in a car with the gas pedal down to the floor because it's vital to the solution of the problem that he reach a particular place at a particular time —and suddenly he's halted at a railroad crossing while a long freight train moves slowly and agonizingly past. This is a legitimate complication because it does make things look blacker— the lead will fail to overcome the problem if he doesn't reach that certain place on time. On the other hand, if it doesn't matter whether he gets there in a few minutes or a few hours, the freight-train incident should not be used as a complication at all—because it becomes pointless. Without a time limit coupled to the basic problem, it doesn't affect the problem in any way, or make things look blacker; all it does is slow down, or stop, the story you're telling.

Because many writers don't actually realize that the only purpose of complications is to increase suspense by making the solution possibilities appear darker and darker, they use an unsatisfactory complication—the reasonless complication, to give it a name—and make a common error. When the lead character must see another character as a possibility of solving his problem in the reasonless-complication stories, the other character is always away or hard to find at first. Actually, this doesn't accomplish a thing toward the building of suspense: on the contrary, it is only the meeting with the other character and the discovery that the interview with him doesn't help solve the problem that makes the solution possibilities look blacker. And when the lead must go somewhere, transportation is always slow or difficult to find—which is exactly the wrong tack, because it's only when the lead gets there and is unsuccessful in his solution attempt that the problem grows grimmer.

Be careful about those complications of yours. Weigh each one painstakingly before you use it. And if you find that it only delays matters a little instead of making things materially worse, don't use it at all. It will do your script more harm than good.

Most reasonless complications also suffer from the fact that they are coincidental—and however often coincidences may occur in real life, they always manage to look phony when they turn up in fiction. You may have just finished drinking two quarts of water the first time anyone ever offered to buy you an ice cream soda, come down with the mumps the day you were supposed to go to the first party in your life at which you were sure there'd be kissing games, and tripped and broken your hipbone as you were rushing from the church with your new mate to go to the honeymoon hotel; but throw these instances of bad luck at a lead character in a book, and the public will find them difficult to swallow. You can get by with an occasional bit of coincidence, such as the passing-freight-train complication—it is, of course, a bit coincidental that the train just happened to be passing at the moment the hero just happened to pass that point at a time when he just happened to be in a terrific hurry—but you can keep coincidence from showing up *too often* by making sure that almost all your complications occur because they're the only things that *could* logically occur as the result of the lead character's unsuccessful efforts to solve his problem.

Another way to avoid the boring and the movement-stopping in your complications is to be careful that your problem does not suggest an enormous number of solution possibilities. This error usually results in the kind of script wherein the problem is not too difficult, but the lead just can't seem to get it solved no matter how hard he tries. He sees one person after another and does one thing after another—all to no avail.

First of all, you're violating a basic rule of problem selection when you choose one of this sort, because the problem must look insoluble to grip the reader's attention—and he won't wait around long enough for the complications to start if the basic problem looks as though it will be a cinch to solve. And secondly, complications on the same level of suspense can grow boring; there's just nothing exciting about one failure to solve after another.

Anything can grow tedious through repetition: even a fight to the death, if the same action occurs over and over again. (Hero and villain fight at cliff's edge overlooking ocean, and villain pushes hero over; hero parts the water neatly, swims out, rejoins the villain and fights some more, and the villain pushes him over again; again he swims out and fights some more with the villain, and again the villain pushes him over; and one more swim-out, fight, and dunking. After several of these forcible dunkings, the hero's soaking wet, the villain's shoulders ache from pushing—and the reader's asleep.) The suspense, therefore, must mount steadily: the basic problem should look absolutely insoluble, only one solution possibility should occur at a time, each attempt to solve the problem should be a strong struggle, and each failure to do so should make the problem seem all the harder to solve.

Make use of your limits when planning your complications: the time limit ("If I don't find the document by nine o'clock, I'm lost"), and the solution-possibilities limit ("If *this* doesn't win Jane back, I'm sunk"). Limits make things more difficult for your lead character, and that is your job in the fiction business.

12

THE FINAL SANDBAG
The Crisis Point

One of the staff editors at my agency defines the problem as the first heavy sandbag that hits the lead character and knocks him to the ground, the complications as additional sandbags that pin him more and more tightly to the ground, and the crisis as the time when one final sandbag completes the pinning down so thoroughly that it seems certain he can never get out from under.

Each new complication in a script makes the situation blacker, but there is always, when the lead recovers a little from the shock of the new complication and peers into the darkness, a faint ray of light and hope—something else he can try that may solve his problem. The sandbags are heavy on his back, but he can still, perhaps, flex his muscles and force his way out. The final complication, which brings on the crisis, comes when the *last* attempt fails: the time when "this is my last chance; if it misses, I'm finished," and it misses.

It is the time, in the man-versus-the-elements-or-environment script, when the farmer uses the last possible object that may rid his acreage of the locusts, and it doesn't succeed and his farm is doomed. It is the time, in the man-versus-man script, when the hero exhausts or loses his last weapon, and the heavily armed villain moves in for the inevitable kill. It is the time, in the man-versus-himself script, when he knows certainly that he cannot overcome his weakness, or when he makes the final and irrevocable wrong decision or choice. It is, in any kind of script, the highest peak-point of suspense for the reader, because it is the moment of greatest certainty of absolute failure for the sympathetic lead character or (in the reverse skeleton) the moment of greatest certainty of absolute success for the unsympathetic lead character.

Naturally, the certainty is not as certain as all that: the farm is not really lost; death at the villain's hand is not really inevitable; and the wrong choice is not really irrevocable, as the eventual solution shows. It does, however, seem absolutely certain at the crisis point, until the final event in the book comes along; whereas after each earlier complication it merely seemed extremely likely.

Plot construction, considered in that way, is a sort of carefully managed, increasingly loud crying of wolf by the author, with the wolf being the impossibility of solving the problem. Actually the wolf is never there, for the problem *is* solved at the end; but, until the end, the reader is made to believe it is there by the apparent insolubility of the basic problem and by the way the added complications seem to prove that the problem is insoluble. And, fortunately for the writing business, readers—unlike shepherds in the fable—never fail to show up because of all the previous wolf-crying; a good new book or story with a fresh problem and fresh complications will start them worrying about the wolf all over again.

Just as the job of the problem and complications is to make the reader feel that solution is very likely impossible, the job of the crisis is to make him feel *certain* that it is impossible. A new depth of despair, rock bottom, is reached; his worry sinks from "My God, this thing may beat Smith!" to "My God, it has!" Things may have looked bad previously, but at least there was always some possibility to be tried; now things look absolutely terrible, and it seems as though all possibilities are exhausted. With your crisis, you give the reader the ultimate in pain, which makes his relief all the more pleasant when the lead character uncovers one more unexpected avenue and wins through to success.

Remember that differentiation between earlier complications and the crisis. After each of the lead character's efforts end unsuccessfully, and result in complications and general darkening of the situation, he may have to think a bit and then come up with another possibility to try, or he may locate and try another possibility almost immediately. At the crisis point, however, there must seem to be no other possibilities left, and therefore the struggle of conjuring up the final possibility and solving the problem must be the strongest struggle in the entire script. It is always a good idea to have each new possibility come hard to the lead character, because it builds suspense—though don't confuse this with the error of delays that keep the lead from coming to grips with the possibilities once he thinks of it—but the last one must come hardest of all.

The script, in other words, must actually *reach* a point where no possibilities are evident, and where the final possibility, which causes the solution, is pretty well hidden until the lead character finds it. You can't just describe the lead character as beaten when the reader can precede you and see a way, or a number of ways, in which he isn't beaten at all. If your script reaches what you believe to be the crisis point, and you sink your lead into the temporary despair that precedes his last and successful effort, you won't make a very good impression on the reader who thinks, "Why, what's wrong with that fool, anyway? He can still do this, or that, or that." And he won't find much to admire when the lead finally wakes up and solves the problem in a way that had occurred to the reader minutes before.

You can't, therefore, allow your lead character to be defeated in a number of attempts to solve his problem and then, arbitrarily, run him through one additional defeat and call that one the last of the possibilities, the crisis point, when it isn't. That is where your limits come in so handy; you can work up a problem that has a limited number of solution possibilities (plus one that you make sure is chosen carefully enough so that the reader can't easily anticipate it), and then reach your crisis point when all the possibilities except the one you've saved have been exhausted. Thus you have a satisfactory crisis—

because it really looks as though your lead character is sunk—and you still have a good, unpredictable solution possibility on hand to use for the finish.

Your lead character must be at the lowest depth of despair at the crisis point: even in the books that go on to end unhappily. In the ultraliterary novel previously described, for example, where the story ends with the lead character's decision that You Can't Win, he is at a lower ebb at the crisis because he is most deeply confused and bewildered, and not yet (as he is at the end) more or less settled by being resigned to his fate.

Never force your crisis; it must be the inevitable result of the preceding events in the script. Assure its inevitability by making your basic problem extremely difficult to solve, and by using every event in your script to make it become more difficult. If every event pushes your lead character deeper and deeper into a pit, it is inevitable that he will eventually touch bottom—and that is your crisis point.

I would like to stress once again—and I can't do it too often —that the lead character's failures at his efforts to solve the problem, which move the script toward the crisis point, must be logical, natural, and "the things that would happen under those circumstances." If you find that the only way you can complicate matters for your lead character is by having him do something illogical or stupid, toss out that complication and think some more until you have one that makes matters worse *despite* the fact that the lead behaves intelligently and events occur naturally. Your reader departs the moment your character acts stupid; he is no longer in sympathy with him. He also departs the moment your characters acts illogically or events occur unnaturally (such as a big coincidence or too many little ones); he no longer believes the book at all.

Whenever possible, make the problem so difficult that the solution possibilities are uncertain and off-chance at best, so that the lead character's failures will be logical, and won't reflect unfavorably on him. The script will also, of course, move smoothly and inevitably to the crisis if the solution possibilities fail in rapid succession.

Keep your script at the crisis point just long enough to convince the reader thoroughly that the lead character is defeated and the problem will not be solved. Then, just as soon as he's convinced, show him he's wrong by sending the lead character zooming up the final stretch to the solution.

13

AND THAT DID THE TRICK
The Solution

This is a true story that has become one of the industry's favorite anecdotes.

Magazines today won't purchase and print a serial as the author completes each installment; they've seen so many good stories fall apart at the end that it is now the rule to see and okay the full script before they begin to publish any part of it. Some years ago, however, many magazines made it a regular practice to rush into print each installment of a novel as the author pulled it out of his typewriter, and the editors of one of these publications found themselves rather worried one day.

They'd just published the next-to-last installment of a novel, and the author had left the lead character, whom we shall call Lance O'Neill, in quite a fix. After a long series of narrow escapes from death at the villain's hands, the crisis had arrived—and it looked as though Lance was really finished this time. He'd fallen into a deep pit set up by the villain, a pit with sides so smooth it was obvious he wouldn't possibly be able to scramble up again. Sharp spikes were beginning to come out of the sides of the pit to impale him and, to make things worse, molten lead was beginning to pour out of a pipe in the pit and fill it up.

The more the editors thought about it, the more it worried them. What if the author couldn't think of a solution—some way to rescue O'Neill: What if he found he just couldn't go on, and they had to publish the next issue without the final installment? The thought was terrible. Thousands of readers might cancel their subscriptions in protest, or even visit the editorial offices personally and carry bullwhips with them.

Frantically they phoned the author at his home, but he wasn't there. They were running down the list, and phoning places at which he might be found, when he walked in. "What's all the excitement about?" he asked.

"The Lance O'Neill novel," the editor-in-chief said nervously. "The predicament he's in—how'd you handle it? Were you able to get him out of it?"

Casually the author took the manuscript of the final installment out of an envelope and pointed to the opening line. This is what it said:

"With a mighty leap, Lance O'Neill sprang out of the pit."

You'd have quite a time trying to sell your stuff today if you finished up with solutions of that sort. It is the perfect example of the big build-up that leads to the big letdown.

It's a bit difficult to imagine what the motives of the author of the Lance O'Neill saga may have been in solving his problem in that way. It makes a wonderful little anecdote, but it's incredibly inexpert plotting technique. Perhaps the circumstances made the sale so certain that he just didn't give a damn; perhaps, like the writers of that movie described in Chapter Eleven, he had written himself so deeply into a jam that he could see no other way out. But whatever his motives, he certainly did not expect his readers to believe that O'Neill could spring out of a pit, however mighty his leap, that had been described as too deep and steep to climb.

Aside from giving the publishing field an anecdote to cherish, Lance O'Neill's mighty leap accomplished only one thing: it splashed vanishing cream over the reading audience and made it disappear. An audience will always leave a novel that it has ceased to believe; it will depart in an annoyed mood when it does not believe the solution, because that's the moment for which it has been waiting ever since the book began. To hold your reader by building up and building up a problem, and then have the lead character resolve it through unbelievable, illogical, or downright silly means, is to give the reader insult, injury, and a hard kick in the pants.

Believability, then, is the first thing for which to watch when you are mapping out your solution. You discard it when you do any of these things:

1. When the lead character solves his problem by doing something that is obviously beyond his powers, as in the O'Neill opus. A good script gives an accurate gauge of a character by his activities throughout; you begin to know the things he can do and cannot do, his exceptional qualities, and the qualities he lacks. He must, therefore, resolve his problem by means that are possible, by an act of which he is capable. Certainly he must make a superior effort to do so after the crisis—certainly he must put everything he has into it—but he cannot, without reason, suddenly be capable of doing things he could not do before.

2. The problem must remain as difficult as ever throughout his solution activities; it must not miraculously be simplified for him. The O'Neill story, looking at the other side of the coin, is bad in this way, too: because, if you are to believe that O'Neill could spring out of the pit, then it must not have been as deep as it had seemed. In that case, the basic problem itself is weak —for the pit was the pièce de résistance, the culmination and the crowning of all the villain's evil attempts on O'Neill's life. If the villain can't do better than a shallow pit from which a man can jump, he's not so tough that he's worth worrying about.

The same principle and objection apply to all other examples: such as the book in which the inexperienced tenderfoot is forced into a gun battle with a quick-drawin' hombre and, amazingly, outdraws him (only to discover afterward that the quick-drawin' villain had injured himself while scratching the small of his back a few minutes before). The reader will find it difficult to believe that Fate, which has buffeted the lead character around all through the book, will suddenly decide to be so good to him at the crucial moment. The lead may, of course, push the odds on his side through his own efforts: for example, by setting the location of the gun duel so that the blinding sun shines in the villain's eyes and his own vision remains clear.

3. Likewise, any other solution by means of sudden good fortune or accident will be eyed dubiously; the sudden arrival of the rich and check-bestowing uncle from 'Mwbongo, a wealthy suburb in Tanzania, or the sudden observing of a thick lump in the mattress that turns out to be a cache stashed away and then forgotten by the room's previous occupant (the exact amount, $837.56, that the lead needs).

There's only one way in which unexpected good fortune, or the unexpected appearance of a new talent or ability on the part of the lead character, can be *handled credibly:* when an earlier clue or plant reveals that the good fortune or talent might have been unexpected by the reader, but not by the lead himself. If, for example, Lance O'Neill had mentioned casually, while leaping over a mud puddle in an early part of the story, that he had won all field events during the last Olympic Games, it would have been more credible when he had leaped out of that pit (stating meanwhile that he had once done three inches better at the standing high jump at college).

The big headache about plants, of course, is that they must be inserted visibly enough so that the reader will say, "Hey, that's right," when the lead uses his special ability, or when the good fortune occurs, and it's revealed to have been foreshadowed; and yet not obviously enough so that the reader will spot it and yawn in bleak anticipation when the crisis point arrives and the lead begins the action toward the solution. The best way to accomplish it is to plant the fact that the lead has the special ability, or has begun to turn the wheels that may bring him the later good fortune, as a part of an earlier effort to solve his problem, so that the reader will not suspect that it will have later significance. It's a touchy business; study lots of plants in published books before you try one yourself.

4. The too-pat solution, where so many things turn out right that it goes beyond the realm of possibility. If your lead character is an escaped con who has broken loose just to murder an old enemy, and in the end understands the error of his ways—due to his love for a girl he's met—and goes back to prison, there's no need for the warden to like him suddenly and turn his back so that the lead can escape again to live happily with the girl, or for the governor to rush forward with a pardon. You see this in new writers' scripts all the time: the lead solves his problem, and immediately the entire world seems to sense it, and everybody acts like a sympathetic character out of the Oz stories. The lead in the prison story has redeemed himself, and will presumably get together with the girl when he finishes his term; but you can bet that he'll have to finish it, and probably serve several additional years as well, as added time for the escape. Solve the problem, certainly, but don't break out into a gigantic rash of good fellowship and have everybody else in the script, even the unsympathetic characters, begin to act like Santa Claus.

Plausibility is one important consideration in planning your solution; proper selection is another.

The all-important purpose of the solution is that it must settle the problem in the most logical and most satisfying way possible—it must take the final step that moves the script to its most suitable destination.

As I've explained earlier, this does not mean that the solution must always be the one the lead character most desires; not at all. It must, however, always be the one that is most logical in view of the earlier occurrences in the story, and that most logically settles the problem.

Sometimes the book *must* end unhappily—or with a mixture of sadness and happiness. (Lead loses his child, despite his frenzied efforts to save her during her illness, but the basic problem is solved—his struggles bring him and his wife together though they had begun to drift apart.) Sometimes a book must end indefinitely. (For example, lead breaks up with his wife because he believes he is in love with a younger woman, later returns to his wife. It would be illogical, and unnatural, if she takes him back at once and their life together immediately resumes its normal course. This book must end indefinitely to end logically; the reader *must* be left only with the hope that things will eventually be the same again.) Sometimes a book will end with the problem completely overcome and eliminated; sometimes it must end with the problem still unbeaten—but settled in the sense that the lead now understands it and is prepared to fight it forever if necessary, or is resigned to it and will try to live happily despite its unremovable presence.

The book that ends with the problem overcome and eliminated is perhaps most easily salable, but any of these types of solutions is good if it is the *right* solution. Don't force an unhappy ending because you've had an argument with your husband or wife and feel morbid that day; or tack on an illogical and contrived happy ending just because you think it is the thing to do. Let the solution stem from the rest of the plot; if it is satisfactorily and irrefutably the only solution that could logically come from the problem and the other events in the script, it is *right*.

I've already said a thing or two about the importance of resolution of the problem through the lead character's own efforts; let me say just a little more.

The important thing is that you do not show the lead up as so weak-charactered that he sits around numbly while someone else solves his problem, or so inept that he fails to solve his problem while someone else comes along and succeeds. He must, as I have said, be worthy of the reader's sympathetic attention.

That means that he must be the moving power in the working out of his own salvation; it does not mean that he has to be Superman. If, in other words, he discovers that he can save himself (and, perhaps, the others in his group) from attacking bandits by rolling a huge boulder down the side of a mountain, it doesn't mean that he must pry the rock loose and heave it downward all by himself; he can get help from the others, but he should be the one to think of the boulder. If he succeeds in locating the gang of twenty killers in a deserted warehouse on the edge of town, he doesn't have to play the comic-magazine hero by attempting to capture them all single-handed, which might make readers scorn his good sense as easily as it might make them admire him. He can call the police, and perhaps later have a solo fight with the chief villain, whom he catches trying to sneak out of a secret exit; the important thing is that he has worked his own salvation by locating the killers and getting them captured.

Don't go out of your way to have your lead character act so heroic that he's unbelievable; but don't let him sit around like a brachycephalic while others work for him, either.

Throughout these past few chapters, which discuss the plot skeleton in detail, you've noted, I trust, that there are a great many holes into which your foot can slip. That, I think, answers better than anything else the question of how much prewriting planning is necessary.

The better your plot plan before you begin writing—the more closely you have checked each of the many considerations that come up in the writing business—the better your chances of producing a good and publishable script. As far as I'm concerned, such book-planning practices as writing up long life histories of each character are nonsense, because I cannot see where they help in any way. But it is a good idea to plan your plots thoroughly and carefully enough so that you don't waste your writing time on scripts that won't sell.

14

WHO TELLS IT?
Viewpoint

Back around 1880, one of the most popular methods of story-telling was the omniscient-viewpoint method, also known as the author-intrusion method. Viewpoint in fiction simply means the person through whose eyes and other senses the action is seen, and the omniscient viewpoint featured the author as a sort of official and visible narrator who described the characters' actions and stepped in and analyzed their emotions or made other comments whenever he felt it necessary. As a result, the reader would get paragraphs like this:

> Genevieve looked up into the handsome stranger's glittering black eyes. "Very well, sir," she said. "I'll come up to your apartment tonight to discuss my new job as your secretary." Alas, poor Genevieve! Your heart flutters only in anticipation of your new job, and not because you are aware that you are in danger. Be careful, innocent Genevieve! The handsome stranger is not the impersonal, kindhearted gentleman he seems!

The author would also stop the action on occasion to moralize or make a direct comment to the reader:

> Van Stuyvesant lurched drunkenly toward her. Demon Rum, that evil beast which inflames men's minds, had taken hold of his senses. O liquor, that terrible and foul master! Better that you, good reader, may never know its horrors.

The omniscient-viewpoint script still turns up on the unrush piles (and, subsequently, in the rejection baskets) at publishing offices all the time. The old-fashioned language is gone, and the author may not sink into coy vapors at each minor

moral misstep, but he is still around to nudge the reader famil-
iarly every once in a while and interpret or comment upon the
characters' actions. A paragraph from a modern omniscient
novel might read something liké this:

> Roberts walked briskly toward the general manager's office.
> He'd have been better off if he'd left well enough alone and stayed
> out the matter entirely, as he was to find out, but he wasn't
> experienced enough to realize it then. He knocked on the door.

There are two important things wrong with the use of the
omniscient viewpoint in fiction. The first is that a good book
holds the reader because it gives the temporary illusion of
reality while he's reading it—because he believes it and gets
engrossed in it during the reading—and the intrusion of the
author or the author's comments snaps him out of it each time
and reminds him that it is, after all, just a story. Frequently,
as in the example given, the author's intrusion describes the
shape of things to come, and there's no better way to destroy
the illusion of reality than to remind the reader that future
events are all mapped out and ready to be brought onstage.

And the second fault of the omniscient viewpoint is that its
author-intrusion characteristic does not help the script in any
real way, but tends instead to distract. Where the author describes the emotions of the characters, it would be better to
show the characters feeling those emotions and thus cause the
reader to know and understand them; where the author comments on the results of their actions, it would be better to let
the script show the results. The best place, in short, for the
author is off the set pulling invisible puppet strings, not on the
set, directing so much attention to himself that the readers
must keep looking away from what the characters are doing.

Shortly after the omniscient viewpoint began its decline
and fall, the observer viewpoint came in for a certain amount
of popularity. This is the type in which the story is told by an
observer or narrator, who usually takes no part or only a minor
part in the events.

Most of the older observer-viewpoint narratives were "frame" stories; that is, the author drew a sort of picture frame around them by including a little introductory scene before the plot proper and a little closing scene after it. The usual frame was one in which a number of people sat around talking, hit on a particular topic, and then one of the people told a tale (the plot proper), which illustrated the topic of discussion; after which the manuscript returned to the conversationalists and they made concluding remarks. Most of P. G. Wodehouse's earlier Mulliner and Oldest Member stories are frame stories, and Joseph Conrad's *Lord Jim* is a classic frame novel.

Frame narratives have pretty much vanished from the current literary scene because of one obvious fact—since the frame is almost always nothing more than an introduction to and a concluding comment on the plot proper, the script is better off without it. All the frame does is hold up the arrival of the real story, and then hold the reader for an unnecessary moment after the real story is over. The form vanished because of the modern trend toward getting the story in motion as early as possible. It will undoubtedly stay away.

And, for exactly the same reason, the nonframe observer story—which hasn't got the elaborate build-up, but still starts with a narrator announcing he's going to tell a story about someone else (for example, "I'll never forget the day young Joe Delaney first hit town")—is objectionable. However short the narrator's opening remarks, even if only one or two lines, they are still unnecessary or in the way—because the story doesn't really start until attention focuses in full on the lead character, the man about whom he's talking. Things would be far better off if the observer were left out entirely and the story begun at once with the appearance of the lead character. Furthermore, the observer viewpoint always keeps the reader from getting to know the lead character quite as well as he might; for the observer, being human, can only describe the lead character's emotions as he assumed them to be from outward appearances "when the events occurred." He cannot, as a directly told narrative may, look right into the lead character's mind.

The best way to tell your story is directly and entirely from the lead character's viewpoint, so that everything that occurs in the script is seen and heard and felt emotionally and judged by the lead character. Remember that your chief hope in writing your scripts is that you'll make your reader identify so closely with the lead character that he'll almost join him in fighting his problem and living the events. It's logical, obviously, that you stand the best chance of accomplishing this if your manner of narration of the occurrences parallels the manner in which life occurs: this is, with the lead character (you or me) always onstage, and knowing of events that occur offstage (away from us) by hearing or being told of them.

Your reader is used to the movement of life in this manner; he can more easily identify himself with the lead character and follow him when the lead character's life moves in the same way. When, however, the script—which is the life the reader is living temporarily if he is identifying with the lead character —follows the lead and his emotions only occasionally, and keeps switching off to events in which the lead does not appear or which he is not observing (however pertinent they may be to the lead's problem), the movement becomes unnatural and the tight chain of reader identification is broken. In real life, there is no switching off of consciousness while things away from one's vision are taking place. Exactly the same thing applies to scripts that delve into the lead character's emotions, but delve into all the other characters' emotions as well—that is, they don't just describe the hero's emotions and *indicate* the other characters' emotions by the lead character's observations of their actions and reactions, but leap nimbly from one character's thought to another. Easy identification with the lead character is barred to the reader when he knows all those thoughts, because it is obvious that the lead character cannot know them.

When the scene shifts without the lead character shifting along with it, or things are revealed in the script whose knowledge the lead character cannot possibly share, the mechanics are showing—it is obviously a story. And full identification is possible only when the reader is made to forget for a while that he's reading a story and thinks he's living a life.

Many new writers are distressed when they are advised that shifting or multiple viewpoints should be avoided, and yet that advice is as sound as it is valuable. The greatest distress results from the fear that these *must* be used: what else does one do when a scene is needed and the lead character cannot be present? Well, the answer is that you gotta when you gotta; if the script cannot possibly be written without occasional shifts away from the lead character's viewpoint, you have no choice but to shift away. Most of the time, however, some careful, logical juggling in your plotting will put your lead character onstage always—which, as the most important character in your script, is where he should really be if you can manage it.

One other type of viewpoint that is dangerous is the objective viewpoint, as used in some of Ernest Hemingway's stories —where the emotions of the lead character and the others in the story are not described or touched upon at all, and only a straight and objective job of reporting is done. Sometimes, as in the Hemingway stories, the events are so dramatic, and the participants' reactions to them so obvious, that a straight reporting job will suffice. Frequently, however, the reader will react emotionally because the character reacts emotionally. Emotion is part of your stock in trade; why avoid it?

There are two reasons why it is preferable that you use third-person more often than first-person. One is that far more third-person novels are bought and published than first-person; the other is that the first-person form is extremely restricting.

You can describe the lead character's physical appearance in third-person scripts. You can show his emotional reactions through his physical reactions (for example, *his face grew red with anger; his lips whitened with fear; hate showed in her eyes; his expression was bleak and icy; his lips twisted with bitterness, and so on*). When a first-person lead character describes his physical appearance, however, or describes too often his own physical or emotional reactions, he sounds either unnatural or self-centered.

About the only time first-person storytelling is preferable to third-person is when the fact that the script is being told in the lead character's own idiom or unusual manner of speech characterizes him more deftly or accurately. You can, for example, build up a character as tough or ruthless by his actions and dialogue in third-person scripts, but sometimes the fact that he does *all* the talking in a first-person script—so that, in effect, you're characterizing him with every line—will accomplish this more strongly. In almost all other cases, the third-person method is preferable.

The other forms—second-person, tales told in the plural—are trick types that you'll see once in an ultramarine moon. Do them as often. Scripts told in letter or telegram form belong in the same category, but more so. Editors once considered this an original and clever method of storytelling, but it has been done so often through the years that the form is unpopular today.

15

WHAT MAKES THEM TICK?
Motivation

Recently, a man in Seattle walked into a restaurant and ordered a porterhouse steak, rare. When the steak was brought, he called for the proprietor and complained that the steak was too well done. The proprietor looked at the steak and insisted it was rare. They argued back and forth for a moment, and abruptly the customer concluded the discussion by seizing his knife and stabbing the proprietor through the heart.

Recently, a Cincinnati woman left for Reno to file suit to divorce her husband. This action stunned her friends, who had thought that the couple were extremely well matched and well adjusted and happy. The woman explained that her husband was a good man and admirable and lovable in almost every way, but he had been entirely too mean to her cat.

Recently, a wealthy and attractive widow in a small town in Illinois chose a husband from among a number of men she'd been seeing. All of them were nice and she had had a terrible time choosing, so, she told a local reporter quite seriously, she finally chose So-and-so because he had such wonderful taste in ties.

These are real-life motivations for murder, divorce, and marriage. All these incidents actually happened; all were reported as oddities during a television newscast. Try to use them in a script, however, and see how far you get.

They are not necessarily studies in abnormal psychology or behavior, either. Court records, news magazine files, and everyday gossip are jam-packed with stories of everyday people, otherwise quite normal and rational, who have done one crazy thing in their time. That includes you and me. You and I, undoubtedly, have never murdered anyone in a fit of pique— at least I haven't, and I hope *you* haven't—or undertaken such major steps as marriage or divorce for such minor reasons, but all of us have done a few things in our lives that we'd admit (to ourselves, anyway) are atypical or odd. The cliché experts have an answer for it; they say, shrugging, that people are people.

Well, people may be people and sometimes do funny or irrational things, but the people in your scripts cannot because they must be "typical" people. Let me show you what I mean.

When a person in real life does something strange, or without an adequate motive or reason, you may be startled by it or wonder about it—but there is no possibility that you will disbelieve it, because you know that it *has* happened. A character in a script, however, is in another situation entirely: let him do something incredible or without adequate motivation, and the reader immediately realizes that the whole thing is made up and doesn't believe any of it.

Let us say that your cousin Hortense married her husband mostly because she just loved the way he whistled the music from *Fiddler on the Roof,* and so you have the heroine in your script select her mate because she loves his skill at whistling. Your readers, however, do not know your cousin Hortense, and it's extremely unlikely that they know anyone who chose a husband on the basis of his whistling skill. Therefore, they don't believe this motive because they don't know it once really happened, and because it is certainly not a typical motive for mate choice—just as you would not believe many real-life occurrences if you did not know for sure that they actually happened.

You're not just telling a little true occurrence to your friends, relatives, and others who are likely to take you at your word; when you're writing a book, you're writing something that, if it sells, will be read by thousands or even millions of people. All kinds of people—farmers and city types and office workers and pick-and-shovel laborers; the innocent who'll believe almost everything, and people who must be convinced before they'll believe *anything*. In order to give your characters adequate and believable motivation for everything they do, therefore, you must give them the most typical and logical motivation—the thing *most* people would do under those circumstances.

That makes the motivation believable at once: why should the character's reason for doing something be incredible when anybody would do what he's doing under similar circumstances? It is only when the character's motives and actions are different from the norm—when he does something for an inadequate reason, or when he does exactly the opposite of what a normal person in that position might be expected to do—that it is disbelieved. The fact that a few people in real life may have acted that way doesn't alter things; you're not going to be able to hand out a signed affidavit to this effect with each copy of the book.

There's a technical name for it: the factor of mass reasoning versus individual reasoning. It is another way of saying the same thing—reasons for particular actions are believable when they are what the mass, the majority of people, would do under those circumstances, and they are not necessarily believable because a few scattered individuals may have done things that way.

People generally act in character. If a weak and cowardly man should walk into a bank and see that it's being held up, he would probably faint, not leap forward unarmed and attack the *banditti*. On a number of occasions in real life, perhaps, some peculiar chemistry may have caused normally cowardly individuals to reverse themselves under stress and turn into tigers—but an unmotivated character change of this sort will rarely be acceptable in fiction.

When you develop a character along specific lines, as you always must—when you show him to be a particular kind of person—his motivations throughout, his reasons for doing whatever he does in the script, must be exactly in line with the way most people of that type would act under those circumstances. If he is built up throughout as a brave man and no hint is ever given to the fact that he's really a phony and a coward underneath it all, it will be unbelievable if he suddenly, without reason, begins to act cowardly. If you build up a character as a timid person who turns pale every time he has to cross a busy intersection because he's afraid he might get hurt, you can't suddenly, for no visible reason, have him change to an intrepid person who grins as he turns to face an escaped lion and, never pausing in his crocheting, kicks the lion all the way back to the circus grounds. (The real-life man who changed under stress from cowardice to heroism may have done so, perhaps, because fear brings a double dose of adrenalin. This isn't adequate reason for the change in fiction, however; adrenalin can also help a frightened man run away twice as fast.) Your motivation, in short, will be sound only if the character always acts typically—always acts like the kind of person you have shown him to be.

This does not mean that your characters need ever be stock types, out of familiar molds; and it doesn't mean that the events in the script need ever be routine. If you really understand the people in your script and are completely positive about the way they would act and react under various circumstances, you may make them as unusual, or their adventures as unusual, as you wish. All that is important is that they remain consistent throughout. The reader will certainly know it if they don't, even though he may never have run across circumstances exactly like those in real life.

If, for example, you want to write a script that ends with a scene in which the hero turns on an escaped lion and pushes him back into his cage, you may certainly go ahead and do so —provided you have built up your hero as a fearless fellow who has grown up among lions (his father was a zookeeper) and knows just how to handle them. The point again is consistency of action, typical action; a brave man with that background might well do what the hero does. It would only be unconvincing if the intersection-fearing character acted that way when confronted by a lion; but it doesn't look ridiculous when, let us say, Tarzan acts that way in films, because Tarzan has been built up believably as a man who does everything but yawn when kings of the jungle menace him. The reader doesn't have to have lion-fighting friends to understand and believe this, or to regard the timid man's lion-shooing as out of character and the courageous zookeeper's son's shooing as believable. If he's ever seen a circus, he knows there are people who can handle lions; on the other side of the coin, he's surely met cowards. Maybe he's even a coward himself; *photos* of lions scare *me*.

Nor does consistency in motivation mean that books that include drastic character changes must be unbelievable. On the contrary, there have, of course, been thousands of thoroughly logical and believable books written along those lines. The important thing is that the change must come for strong, well-motivated reasons.

It may come, for example, if the heroine turns bitterly away from the timid lead character, disgusted at his cowardice, and he is *forced* to be heroic because he'll lose her forever if he isn't—as a result of which he discovers that it isn't so hard being a brave man, after all. Or, let us say, the tough, deadly, close-mouthed murderer has one chink in his armor—a pathological fear of rats, established early in the story—and the lead breaks his spirit and makes him confess by locking him overnight in a vermin-ridden cell.

When you do this sort of thing in your script, you aren't causing your people to act *out of* character—you're merely causing them to act in a new way that is acceptable because they've undergone a perfectly logical and reasonable *change* in character. What you've done, in effect, is to put two strong facets of their character at war, and allowed the stronger facet to win. Fear is strong in the timid hero, but his love for the heroine is stronger, and so his character changes—and he bypasses his former mode of action (cowardice) and acts bravely, as his new character demands. Toughness is strong in the villain, but his pathological fear of rats is strong, too—and it becomes the stronger of the two and overpowers the other when the hero magnifies it by forcing the villain to remain overnight in the vermin-filled cell.

If you really understand people as you should, you're familiar with the basic drives that make us act as we do—love, hate, fear, greed, jealousy, the struggle for security, and so on. Use these to motivate your characters, or to cause character change. And make sure, most of all, that you never make your characters act illogically, or do things without adequate reason, just because you want to keep the manuscript rolling.

16

BUT WHO'LL BELIEVE IT?
Plausibility

The means of assuring plausibility in your scripts is an extension or enlargement of the method by which you assure logical and adequate motivation. It is, in other words, the same principle of mass or majority versus individual, applied to everything in your script rather than just to the characters' reasons for doing what they do.

In gauging the logic or adequacy of your characters' motivations, you use the yardstick of whether or not most real-life people would act or react in that way under those circumstances. In gauging the plausibility of things other than motivation in your script, you use the yardstick of whether or not events most usually happen that way, or would most logically happen that way.

Coincidence, for example, is implausible because it is not the way things most usually happen—because, in short, it is the way things may have happened in comparatively rare *individual* real-life cases, but not the way things happen in the *mass* or *majority* of real-life cases. Most people who are in trouble in real life don't get out of it through the receipt of an unexpected big check, or through the fortuitous discovery of a large sum of money in an old mattress at the exact moment of extreme need. Most people who are in trouble in real life just don't have the good luck of seeing the one person who can help them turn up out of the distant past at the crucial moment.

"Good God, prisoner—I'd know that diamond-shaped birthmark anywhere! Aren't you the son of old Yancey Doodle, who used to

be a horse ostler in Memphis? He once gave me two crusts of bread and a dab of peanut butter when I was a starving young lawyer— before I became the famous, well-respected, lovable, distinguished judge I am now. Son, the charges of murder, blackmail, kidnapping, arson, conspiracy to overthrow the government, armed robbery, counterfeiting, forgery, and expectoration in the subway are dismissed!"

Things of the above sort, much modified, *have* happened— the arrival of coincidental good luck at times when it's most needed—but these occurrences are so few and far between that each one usually receives considerable publicity as an oddity. Most of the time, people in real life get out of their troubles through plenty of toil and struggle, and that is the way it must be in fiction.

By the same token, as explained earlier, coincidental *bad* luck is just as implausible—where the complications don't occur as unfortunate but natural results of the hero's efforts to solve his problem, but where they happen without build-up or reason just so things can be tougher for the hero. If the hero, for example, is on his way somewhere to solve his problem and just happens to trip on a loose rock and breaks his leg, the script becomes "contrived"—that is to say, the author is *making* things happen, instead of letting things happen as natural results, as in real life. If, on the other hand, the hero is forced, in order to solve his problem, to climb a shaky structure that he knows may collapse and injure him, and it does and he breaks his leg, there's nothing contrived or implausible about it—it's a natural result.

Few people in real life actually receive what might be called the "Job treatment" by Fate—more and more bad luck just happening to pile up on an original piece of bad luck or trouble. Even those pyramids of minor troubles—those days where everything seems to go wrong—are less often series of coincidences in real life than they are "the unfortunate but natural results of the lead character's efforts to solve his problem." Your basic problem arrives (the alarm clock fails to go off and you may be late for work) and thereafter almost everything else that goes wrong—the burning of the toast, the spoiling of the eggs, the putting on of the wrong suit or dress, etc.—stems from the fact that you're rushing so much to solve your problem and get to work on time that you mess up the other things. And by then, of course, you've put yourself in such a nervous state that you mess up everything else through the day, and magnify the other few annoyances that just happen, when, ordinarily, you'd ignore them.

Dig into your own experience and you'll find that the cases of serious bad luck piled on serious bad luck in real life are so rare that they have become local legends. They certainly aren't sufficiently in the majority, or typical enough, to be plausible in fiction.

Coincidences don't have to be king-size to do injury to your script, either; even little things that just happen to happen can be harmful. The safe just happens to have been left open by mistake the day the hero sneaks into the house to search for the missing papers; the heroine gets lost and just happens to stop for directions at the farmhouse where the villain is hiding out—any event that "just happens" and is too convenient to the story is suspect. When you're about to toss in a too-convenient event on the grounds that, well, it's *possible,* remember that the test of plausibility is not whether or not it's possible; it's whether it's *probable.*

Usually, triteness in a script brings with it a strong odor or implausibility. Coincidence and contrived complications fail to satisfy readers because they seem too obviously invented, or because they lack the necessary aura of reality or real life. In the same way, many trite situations and character types are laughed at today because they've been used so often in stories and have become so heavily identified with fiction that readers no longer associate them with actuality or real life.

There are, I suppose, still some hard-hearted bankers and property owners who heave out tenants if they're fifty-five seconds beyond the final deadline allowed for their mortgage or rental payments, and still a goodly number of young ladies who are told that they may make mortgage or rental payments through the temporary or permanent loan of what is euphemistically known as their honor. There are, I suppose, even a number of cases where people have been murdered or forced to yield up secrets by being tied to railroad tracks while the train loomed not too far in the distance. However, just try to use these little items in scripts today and attempt to get them published. I dare you.

The death of many of these trite items, of course, has been helped along by the fact that people have become, with the spread of communication and entertainment facilities, far more sophisticated in their fiction tastes and their hunt for realism. They know now that many of the "mellerdrammer" situations and character types (in which they once believed so faithfully) never existed at all, or at least not as generally as they had supposed. Even during the financial panics and depressions of the 1870s, 1880s, and 1930s, when a great many people did find themselves homeless, the amount of hard-hearted eviction specialists in fiction was out of all proportion to those in real life, so you might call it the factor of mass versus individual at work again. Some trite items, too, have been given the final push into their graves by changes in custom that altered them from everyday occurrences to rarities; for example, the implausibility today—due to the decrease of parental control over children—of the once quite logical parental-objection complication in romantic fiction. The same applies today to the disappearance of the character who sinks into despair and degradation because she's had an illicit affair and a child out of wedlock; it's gone because many people, including some very famous people, live together today and have children without embarrassment and without a marriage license.

The absent-minded professor was quite acceptable a character in the less critical era; today this fellow who reacts to rainstorms by putting his open umbrella on his head and holding his hat up in the air is generally considered implausible because people measure him against their own teachers and know that extremely few, if any, are that sort of muddleheaded idiot. You'll also note a steadily decreasing number of comic drunks in fiction, because today's more knowledgeable reader realizes that most habitual drunks are frightening or pitiful rather than funny. The same thing applies to yesterday's too positive, too black-or-white types—the Hairbreadth Harry hero who does everything out of innate goodness and the villain who does everything out of innate evil. It's certainly easier to paint a character as all boy scout or all rat, and perhaps there *are* a few people on earth who live only to do good or evil, but most people do what they do for sound personal reasons.

The telltale-personal-characteristics bit has gone down the drain, too. Readers are no longer naïve enough to believe that a man whose eyes are shifty, or who can't look straight at you during a conversation, is necessarily a crook. It may be nothing more than shyness, while the clear-eyed, even-featured chap may pick your pocket while you're busy admiring his clear eyes and even features. And it's hardly necessary, I suppose, to tell you that a mustache is no longer a trademark of villainy, particularly if you happen to wear a mustache yourself.

Accuracy of facts is another important factor in the job of assuring plausibility in your script. There was a time when a little technical mumbo jumbo that *sounded* right would suffice, but not anymore. People are better educated today; mass magazine, book, and paperback book publishing have spread the reading habit; and the various other entertainment media teach things, too. Make one factual misstep today, and hundreds of people will write nasty letters. They'll have learned the correct facts of the matter at school, in other books or stories, in movies or stage plays, or while watching television.

It's bad when an editor catches you in a factual error, and it's downright terrible when he misses it, and readers or critics point it out. He may decide, consciously or subconsciously, that it's dangerous to publish further scripts by a writer as careless as you. As far as the readers are concerned, the misstep may destroy the plausibility of the entire story for them, particularly if it indicates that you don't know the general subject or background about which you're writing, or if the erroneous fact (or incorrectly described gadget) is the means of bringing about the problem, complications, or solution. I'll have a little more to say about accuracy of facts in the chapter on locale.

An individual or atypical occurrence will never be plausible in a script when you attempt to pass it off on the reader as the typical or natural thing that would happen under those circumstances. You may, however, use an individual occurrence if a definite point is made of its individuality, or if that's the entire point of the book.

Let's say that you've learned somewhere that a few dogs have been taught to climb trees. Most dogs, of course, cannot, so a story occurrence would strike the reader as absolutely implausible if a dog had been chasing a cat and proceeded to chase it right up the trunk of a tree. If, however, the character who owns the dog mentions specifically that Rover can climb trees—and does so in such a way (perhaps by naming actual dogs who have climbed trees and received some fame for it) that the reader realizes some dogs *can*—it will not be implausible if an important development later hinges on the dog's upward climb through the branches.

Fantasies are built on the same principle, except that the individual fact is not actually true. The reader gives the author the benefit of one assumption—that, let us say, there *are* werewolves, or space travel to Venus *is* an everyday affair—and the author goes on from there. All the other facts (excepting those concerning werewolves, or travel to or life on Venus, where the author has a free hand) must operate on normal standards of plausibility. The humans must still act like humans, and do things for the reasons most humans do them; all natural events must still happen naturally and logically.

If, then, you decide to do a scene in which a dog climbs a tree, or a scene in which a man knifes a restauranteur because he believes his steak is too well done, you need not necessarily turn out an implausible job—provided definite backing-up and attention are given to the unusualness of the dog's ability and the steak eater's action. You'll go awry only when you ring in that sort of thing without special heralding, in the blind hope that your readers will be dull-witted enough to assume that that's the way those things usually happen.

17

HIS THOUGHTS RETURNED TO HIS CHILDHOOD
Flashback

A friend of mine named John Hartford once had the harrowing experience of finding himself alone with a homicidal maniac in a self-service elevator stuck between floors. Hartford had noticed another man get in the elevator with him as he hurried into his apartment building, but hadn't thought much about it until the creaky old elevator quit abruptly, as it occasionally did, and remained stuck between floors. Suddenly the other man began to mutter hoarsely that my friend was a secret agent and a murderer, and Hartford looked up into the wildest eyes he'd ever seen in his life. As he watched, the man said, "I'll kill you first," and drew a long, thin knife from his pocket.

Hartford's horror grew when he saw that the blade was already bloodstained.

The man began to move slowly toward him and, strangely, something about which Hartford hadn't thought for many years flashed into his mind—his last day in Indiana before he'd left to live in New York. He thought about the turmoil within him that day, the struggle between his love for his hometown and his desire to make good in the big city, and how he might not now be facing death at a madman's hands if he'd decided to stay home. He remembered his Aunt Marian, pleading with him. "John," she'd said that day, "your father says you've definitely made up your mind to go to New York. You mustn't do it, John. I've been in New York many times, and . . ."

Tell me, are you aching to tell Aunt Marian to close her mouth? Are you anxious to go on finding out what happened to Hartford in the self-service elevator that night? If so, I've succeeded in illustrating the chief reason for general editorial objection to the flashback: its stop-the-story aspect.

The human mind acts strangely when its owner is under stress, and the truth is that many thoughts of the past did crowd into Hartford's consciousness in those few seconds—the things his Aunt Marian had said, the things his father and mother had said, the things his Uncle Henry had said, the things he'd said, even some of the details of his train trip East. I could go on telling you about them for the next three or four pages. I won't, however, because I know you're interested in the main story line rather than its sidetracks; I almost knifed Hartford myself when he paused, in telling his experience to me, to describe in minute details his fevered reminiscences as the demented man came closer to him. Anyhow, to get back to it, Hartford is six feet four and weighs 240 pounds, so he hit the other man with all his strength. The man went down, which enabled Hartford to get out of the elevator and summon the police.

As in this little true story, flashback has earned its bad reputation because, too often, it interrupts the exciting here-and-now events to fill in background or tell some incident in past history that is neither absolutely relevant nor anywhere nearly as exciting. The reader, naturally, doesn't like this, because he has become interested in the here-and-now events— the things that are happening at present in the book—and he wants to go on seeing how things in the here-and-now turn out. As far as he's concerned, therefore, the flashback is merely an annoying interruption, and he may either skip it entirely or skim through it rapidly and apathetically so that he can get back to the interesting things that are happening *now*.

Let's take an example. Let's take a marriage-problem novel in which the heroine and her husband have had a lot of little arguments, but she's always shrugged these off as unimportant and normal until he tells her bluntly one day that he's sick of their constant bickering and has begun to see another woman. After he leaves, she stands there numbly, wondering what she's going to do. She still loves him very much, but she cannot bring herself to try to win him back in view of this certain proof that he no longer loves her.

All right, the reader's on board. He likes the heroine, and he likes her husband, and he thinks they're both a little at fault, and he'd like to see them get together again. It doesn't look as though it will be easy, and his attention is held as he watches the heroine begin to struggle with her problem. But what do you know? Unhappily, the writer has the flashback disease.

So the heroine stands there numbly for a moment, and then a flashback begins. Her thoughts wander and she begins to remember happier days . . . when she first met her husband . . . the first few times they went out together . . .

Perhaps the way in which they met was mildly amusing. They'd both gone into a bookshop to buy a popular new novel, and she got there first and picked up the only copy left, and he wanted it and was rather angry. And then, after a while, they began to talk . . . and had lunch together, and that night he apologized for his boorishness by sending her a complete set of the author's works. Since then, through the years, he has always brought home two copies of each new book by that author, and they always laugh about it.

Nice stuff. Maybe even, if the writer is skillful, heartwarming stuff. But honestly, what has it got to do with the problem?

Little touches of this sort are fine; they help point up the urgency of the problem by underlining the fact that their love was once a beautiful thing and it would be a great pity for it to end now. But many writers don't confine themselves to little touches; they break out in full-blown flashback and give the reader a long, drawn-out, detail-by-detail history of the past. The result is that the reader is annoyed by it, or his interest is lessened, because it takes him away too long from seeing what is happening to the interesting and urgent problem right now.

Or take another example: the story of a young rancher who discovers that his cattle are being rustled. His thoughts slide back to the past, and the following scenes detail his hardships while pioneering through the West and slowly building up his herds of cattle. Again that sort of thing has some point, because the importance of the problem is underlined by the fact that he had so hard a time getting his ranch and the cattle in the first place. This detailed flashback misses its purpose, too, however, because it takes so long to give added proof of the *urgency* of the problem that it keeps the reader away from his main interest: the story of what is being done to *solve* the problem. It is, in a way, like talking so much to convince a friend that you must borrow his car to get somewhere by three o'clock that you finish your summing-up at four.

So many writers misuse flashbacks and turn them into boring dead-stops-in-the-story-movement that editors have become wary of flashbacks in any shape or form. One or two even state morosely that they think writers are better off if they never use flashback at all.

Actually, of course, that just isn't possible, as even the most morose editors will admit when they're discussing writers who use flashback properly. There are a number of instances where flashback, correctly used, is a good thing, and vitally necessary.

One of these is the build-up-the-urgency use, as discussed, when done properly. Another is when past events are needed to explain current action: why the hero has come to this particular town to solve his problem, or why the hero is in jail when the book opens with an escape scene. And a third is when an important past occurrence has a definite effect on here-and-now action; when, for example, the hero displays great fear in approaching a fight with the villain because he has a psychological horror of boxing—the result of an accident years ago in the ring at the YMCA that resulted in the death of his friend.

When it's at all possible, try to start your script at the beginning (approximately around the time of the arrival of the basic problem) and follow events chronologically through to the ending (the solution of the problem). That is the simplest way to keep your story line direct, and avoid boring and action-stopping explanations of the past. Sometimes, as I've said, it isn't possible. In some books where a past event has a definite effect on current events, it would be foolish to start all the way back at scenes of childhood and work up to the adult scenes where the problem first begins. In some books where the lead comes to a strange town and meets his problem, the events that brought him there are not as important or interesting as the event in the town that starts the problem, and it's better to explain the reasons for his trip later on—rather than start in his hometown and include a lot of unncessary stuff before he gets to the new place where the problem begins.

In those cases and others like them, of course, flashbacks are necessary, and then the important thing is the way in which flashbacks are handled.

The best way is the flashback that doesn't look like a flashback. It is, in other words, the method by which important facts of the past are doled out to the reader a little at a time, and carefully integrated with the present action. This is the kind of flashback you should use most of the time, and it will serve all purposes, whatever your reasons for the flashback may be.

Let's take, by way of example, a Western novel by an experienced professional, which we sold to a hardcover house, and then as a television film, a while back. The hero is a blind man who arrives in a strange town and is immediately met by trouble from people who want to keep him out.

The book opened at that point because it was the beginning of his basic problem, but there were two earlier events that had to be covered for clarity of the story and present action. One was the hero's reason for coming to the town; the other was the manner in which he had become blind. The author covered the first of these in a hidden flashback integrated into the scene in which the hero and the heroine first get together in the town:

Then he stopped. The light footsteps he had heard leaving the schoolhouse were running toward him. And when he heard a girl's voice say, "Bill! Bill Andrews!"—the same voice, grown up now, but the same quality of sweetness—he knew it was Lorna Stone.

He turned and said, "Been a long time, hasn't it?"

She was in his arms and her lips touched his before she answered. "Almost eight years," she said. "Eight years—yet you came right away."

"Us blind fellows ain't kept too busy, Lorna," he said softly.

The here-and-now action in this sequence has not stopped for a second, yet the author has included all the salient facts of a past occurrence, or several. The reader has watched an active scene that is important to the story, yet he now knows (a) the hero knew Lorna Stone years ago, (b) presumably when they were children, and (c) he has come as the result of her summons. In a later conversation, there's a completely natural mention of her letter, so the reader knows that this is the form her summons took.

The author establishes the facts of the time the hero became blind in a here-and-now fast-action scene:

The shot came just when he knew it would—the moment he stepped away from the darkened schoolhouse. For a moment, he felt wild, muscle-stiffening fear, the way he had felt as a kid when outlaws killed his mother and dad and fired the bullet which left him alive but blind; and then it passed away. He fell onto his stomach, and his gun leaped forward in his hand.

The childhood occurrence is important to the book because it helps explain his absolute hatred for outlaws, and so the author covers it. By integrating it into the present onstage action of the book, however, he's done it painlessly, and eliminated the necessity of pausing for story-stopping long looks back.

In the same way, flashbacks that don't look like flashbacks can fill the need for comments on the past in any kind of script. The marriage-problem novel, for example, might do it this way:

She walked slowly down the street, and stopped in front of Neil's Bookshop to wait for her bus. The sight of the store increased the heavy, sick pain within her. It was there that they had first met—there that a silly little quarrel over the one remaining copy of a book by their favorite author had ended in lunch together "to talk it over." That night Jim had apologized for his part in the quarrel by sending her a complete set of books by the author. Tears stung her eyes, and she turned away and saw that her bus was coming.

Here again the majority of the salient facts of the past event are interspersed with the action, so that no actual stop of the present story and trip to the past has been made. The remaining fact—that Jim now buys two copies of each book and they laugh about it—can be introduced later in much the same way.

One caution in using flashbacks in this way: don't force them. Don't have your characters think in a peculiar way, or act peculiarly, just so you can get in the necessary past facts. This sort of thing will never do:

She looked out of the window and saw a boy passing. The boy was wearing a sweater. Sweaters are usually knitted, and that reminded her of knitting, and she remembered with a sob that she had first met Joe at a bar, which was two doors down from a knitting store, or was it a pet shop?

As in everything else in fiction, keep it logical. Work at it and you'll find that you always can.

The integrated, bit-by-bit flashback, as described, can be used in almost all cases. Probably the only exception is where the past event is so important to the script, and so dramatic in itself, that you're positive your book will be improved rather than injured if you use a full-size, visible flashback.

In that case, of course, go ahead and use the full-size flashback. Take the curse off it, however, by making sure of two things. First, make it as interesting as you possibly can, so that the reader won't resent so much the pull away from the here-and-now. And second, try to make it seem as little like a flashback as possible by getting rid promptly of the past tenses.

It's not necessary to load your flashback scenes with those reminders that things *have* happened, rather than *are* happening: the "had"s and the "had had"s. The following continues to remind the reader that it's just the past being hashed over:

> She had gone to the study to rest for a few minutes, and had fallen asleep. Dan's soft voice had awakened her suddenly.
> "Kathie," he had said, "wake up—wake up, please."
> She had opened her eyes to see him glaring at her. "What is it, Dan?" she'd asked.
> "Your father's back, Kathie," he had told her.

Eliminate the "had"s as quickly as possible and the scene becomes both easier to read and less a constant reminder that it's flashback.

> She had gone to the study to rest for a few minutes, and had fallen asleep. Dan's soft voice woke her suddenly.
> "Kathie," he said, "wake up—wake up, please."
> She opened her eyes to see him glaring at her. "What is it, Dan?" she asked.
> "Your father's back, Kathie," he told her.

One other type of flashback is the "everything-remembered" variety. This is the one in which, let us say, a woman sits in a chair beside the body of her husband, whom she has just killed, and remembers past incidents in their lives (which take up the bulk of the chapter).

In a sense, this is not as much a flashback as it is a frame. In most of these, more than ninety percent of the chapter takes place during the remembered events. The opening, the occasional brief returns to the present, and the ending usually serve as nothing more than an introduction, intermediate comments, and concluding comments to the remembered events.

There are two things wrong with the everything-remembered script. The first is that it forces the reader to realize throughout that everything has already taken place before the present and has already reached a conclusion, which gives him that subconscious feeling of lack of urgency that comes whenever he realizes that, as I've said before, all the action is already worked out and just waiting to be brought onstage. (It would take a psychologist to figure out why, but no matter what the era in which a book is set, it still generates urgency if the story is told as here-and-now and just happening—even if the era is 1,000,000 B.C. The reader, so to speak, lives in that era while the narrative is going on. Tell him, however, that this event or that took place before the current time of the book, and he feels that that event has "already happened," so why worry about it?)

The second thing wrong with the everything-remembered script is that the sense of urgency is reduced still further because the opening scene "in the present" usually tells how the whole thing is going to turn out. The reader, therefore, is never in the real state of suspense that comes with growing worry over how things are going to finish.

There is only one time when the everything-remembered device is best: when most of the opening events of a plot are rather mild, but build up to a powerful conclusion, and the telling of the conclusion or near conclusion *first* serves to grip the reader. It's always best when you can make it the near conclusion, of course, so some suspense will remain on how it's going to end.

All in all, you'd do well to use this type sparingly; it isn't too popular, for the reasons given, with the reading public.

18

STRANGE SOUNDS AND SMELLS
Locale

I've mentioned several times that anything that halts the steady forward movement of your script, even for a little while, is not good. This also applies, and very much so, to locale and background.

It used to be quite acceptable practice for the author to stop the story action entirely when he felt that some background painting was required, and proceed to sketch in the surroundings and scenery with thick, unrelieved strokes. A few professionals still do it that way. It has never been entirely satisfactory, however, because it's the natural tendency of most readers to shy away from heavy sections of continuous description, and skim them or skip them entirely. You've probably done it yourself on many occasions: the *action* stops suddenly and you're confronted by long paragraphs or even pages of description, and you flip the page or pages and resume reading where the story movement starts up again.

Descriptions of background and locale are important to the success of your book or story. They help build and shape the mood—the happy tone in a scene is always increased when the surroundings seem just as bright and pleasant as the occurrences, and grimness or horror is always emphasized when the events occur in ugly weather and foreboding surroundings—and they help the reader picture the story events by showing him what things look like as well as what is happening. It's a great pity, therefore, when these purposes are defeated because the descriptions are stuck together in such a boring-looking lump that the reader skips it, and most writers today avoid this danger by employing the same principle as that used in the flashback that doesn't look like a flashback. They break up their descriptions of locale and background into small and palatable doses, and integrate them into the action.

Under the one-blob-of-description method, for example, a house might be described in this way:

> Frank paused and looked at the house.
>
> It was a big house, but old, with the look of death and decay about it. It was obvious that it had been standing there for nearly a hundred years, and the paint that had once been white was now yellowish and peeling. Here and there, large strips of paint had peeled off completely, revealing the rough wood underneath. Shutters hung loosely from the windows, and one or two seemed ready to fall. The wood of the stairs leading up to the front door was decayed, and the knocker on the front door was rusty and dirty. All in all, it was quite an ugly place.

The description gives the picture, all right, but it stops the forward motion to do it. The integrated method might handle the same effect this way:

> Frank walked up the stairs, stepping carefully because the wood underneath his feet looked ancient and as though it might cave in at any moment. The whole place looked that way—paint yellowish and peeling, window shutters hanging loosely and ready to fall, a general look of death and decay. It was, he thought sourly, a hell of a house for an intelligent man like John Drexel to buy.
>
> He used the knocker, and his hand came away covered with rust and filth. When the door opened, a sickening odor of dankness filled his nostrils.
>
> He said, "I want to see Drexel."

Actually, the descriptive phrases need not be packed as closely together in the integrated-with-action method; I've done so here only because I want to keep these examples brief. Frank's reactions to the house may continue, piece by piece, all through his visit there, all through his talk with Drexel.

The one-blob use of description is like seeing scenery in a

landscape painting; the other is like seeing it in a motion picture film. In the first, you must make a deliberate stop to see the scenery; in the second, the scenery is introduced unobtrusively while your attention is held by the action. Since the reader's purpose in staying with a book is to watch the action and see how things come out, you can see why he'll prefer the no-stop method.

In these two examples, I've tried, in addition to the discussion of the advantages of integrated description over dead-stop description, to illustrate another important consideration in this matter of locale. To increase the vividness of the reader's picture of the setting, bring all the senses into play whenever possible.

The reader, remember, shares vicariously all the lead character's experiences, and along with them all his reactions, feelings, and sensations. When the lead notes something with only one sense, so, of course, will the reader.

In the first example, Frank's impressions of the house are entirely visual. He sees the house and notes many things about it, and the picture thus conveyed to the reader is moderately vivid.

The pictures conveyed to the reader by Frank's impressions in the second example, however, are far more vivid because several of Frank's senses have been put to use. His reactions to the place this time are composed of equal parts of the way he *sees* the place (the yellowish and peeling paint, the hanging shutters, etc.), the way he *feels* the place through his sense of touch (the sensation of the treacherous stairs swaying underneath his feet, the feeling of rust and filth on his hand), and the way he *smells* the place (the dank odor in his nostrils).

Observation through one sense is often quite vivid: for example, if you see, through the closed window in your room, a youngster hit by a speeding automobile. The vividness is magnified a thousand times, however, if you are on the spot and also hear the thud and the boy's screams, feel blood splash on you, and smell the odor of screeching tires. Scenes in silent motion pictures were sometimes vivid, but there is no comparison to the vivid effects achieved through the addition of sound and color. As a reverse example (sound without vision and then the two together), millions of people, years ago, enjoyed dramas on the radio, but there's no comparison with the effectiveness of television drama, because that is *two*-sense home entertainment. The one-sense radio drama is flat and lacking by comparison because it brought only fifty percent of the reactions that come with hearing *and* seeing a television drama.

The use of as many senses as possible in your scripts, of course, can be overdone; don't have your lead go around stroking everything in sight and sniffing the air like a retired firestation hound as the engine goes by. When, however, a description comes up in which more than just the visual sense can logically and normally be employed, you'll increase the vividness by employing the others as well.

Remember, too, that the reader must know what the lead character or the author is talking about if he's going to share the sense reactions. Some foreign-locale books, for instance, have the lead character's nose twitching happily as he sits by the campfire and smells 'gwobnoogo being cooked. The readers find that sort of reaction hard to share when they don't know what 'gwobnoogo happens to be, or what it smells like. Is it fish —meat of some kind—vegetables—or tree bark? Your lead character should translate and, if the object is peculiar to that locale, compare it to something with which the reader will be familiar. (Example: *"That night I sat at the campfire, my nostrils twitching hungrily as the odor of* 'gwobnoogo, *an African bird that tastes just like turkey, was wafted toward me."*)

Foreign phrases that will be familiar and understandable to the average reader need not be explained. The average person knows what *parlez-vous français?* means, and is aware that *Schweinhund* is not an expression of endearment. Unfamiliar words and phrases, however, should be explained to be understood, either by direct translation or by use in a sentence where the context makes it clear. (Example of direct translation: *"He approached the peasant. 'Magli wah gagli.' he said. 'Let's you and me fight.'* " The English sentence, of course, is a translation of the foreign sentence. This double standard, a foreign sentence always followed by an English sentence, can make tiresome reading after a while, and it's wise to use explanation by context as often as possible: " *'Glunkel!' the chieftain said. Rodgers smiled. 'Thank you for calling me your friend,' he replied, and they shook hands solemnly."* Or: *"The guard rushed into the room, swinging a sharp-bladed* kris. *One swing lopped off Professor Carlisle's head."* You don't need a translator to guess the meaning of *kris.*)

And even in the English language, make sure that your descriptive comparisons are comprehensible to the average reader. It just isn't good sense to show off the fact that you once took a course in advanced bird-watching by comparing something to the shape of a gitchee-bird when seen at twilight, or any other such obscure thing. When something smells like honey, say that it smells like honey, and not like the Persian dittle flower (of which three exist on earth, and which also smells like honey). Your reader won't rush to pick up his encyclopedia and find out what you're talking about; he'll just examine the description uncomprehendingly and pass over it, so you'll miss giving him the vivid and clear picture he should get.

It's not necessary to establish an absolute and definite locale in every script you write. If a story can take place in any town just as easily as in any other, it is not a requirement or particularly essential that you give the locale a name.

If, however, there will be something in the script that *will* identify the locale as a particular one—a specific city such as London (for example, if a scene takes place in Westminster Abbey), or a specific kind of town such as a small town (for example, if some aspect of the plot deals with local farms), or a specific area such as Florida (for example, if it's essential to the plot that the heroine take a sunbath in December)—be sure to establish early in the story that it takes place in that particular town, kind of town, or area. Don't just leave it vague and unstated and then spring it on the reader all at once in the middle of the script.

Unless you name the specific locale or kind of locale almost at the beginning of the script and name any other pertinent and related aspects such as the weather, the reader's natural tendency will be to identify the locale and conditions—while he's identifying the lead character with himself—with his own locale and conditions. If, therefore, he lives in a small town and has read the first dozen pages (in which no locale is named and the action gives no clue) as having taken place in a town like his own town, it will come as a shock and a rift in the reality if your hero suddenly asks the heroine to have lunch with him that night at a little restaurant on the Left Bank. If, in the same way, the sun is shining outside his window as he reads your story, and he automatically and subconsciously assumes that the weather is sunny in the story, it will come as a shock and a disturbance if you suddenly remember to mention on page seven that all the events have been taking place in the pouring rain. The reader will have to adjust his mind back to the beginning, and revisualize all that has gone before as happening in the slightly more frenzied atmosphere of a downpour, and that will pull him out of his semi-hypnotic state of living along with the lead character.

When you choose a specific locale, make sure that you know it well. That does not mean, as I have said, that it *must* be your own locale or one with which you're personally familiar. If you know your locale well enough through study of your encyclopedia, research, discussions with people who've lived there, or the reading of other books about it, it will often suffice. You'd better check all specific statements of fact about the locale, however, and make sure your characters act and speak like the real people who live there. Be careful about regional idioms, local customs, and the like.

But if you don't hate your own locale so much that you can't stand to write about it, why *not* stick to it? Certainly you'll always be safer and more sure-footed that way.

I've already stressed the importance of accuracy in your fiction, and obviously accuracy in matters of locale stands high on the list. You've undoubtedly heard a few examples on the other side of the coin, the most famous perhaps being the fact that early editions of Edgar Rice Burroughs's *Tarzan of the Apes* included tigers among the denizens of the African jungle, and the book did wonderfully well, anyhow. Remember that those examples are famous because they're such rare occurrences. They certainly aren't an excuse for carelessness in your own work.

PART THREE

THE WRITING FACTS

19

LINCOLN'S MOTHER'S DOCTOR'S DOG
The Title

The newspapers once published a story about a noted psychologist, and quoted him as saying that the four words that most easily arouse emotion in Americans are Lincoln, mother, doctor, and dog. This news fired the imagination of one young writer, who immediately wrote a story and topped it with what he described as the most ideal title of all time: *Lincoln's Mother's Doctor's Dog.*

It's not necessary, thank heavens, to go to such extremes to provide ideal titles for your scripts. Your titles don't have to make the reader turn emotional handsprings: all they have to do is be interesting enough to seduce him into reading the book. And that should never be too hard to do, provided you use your good common sense in making your title selections.

The title is an important part of your sales campaign on your book. It is, provided the physical appearance of your manuscript is not so sloppy that it's distracting, the first thing that the editor sees; and, if the book is published, one of the first things the reader examines while he tries to decide whether to buy your book or another one in the store. It must, therefore, always do its job properly.

There are many things that can be wrong with a title. First and foremost in the chamber of horrors is the dull or trite title, which repels rather than attracts the reader because it makes him suspect that the book itself will be just as dull or trite.

Clichés, overworked proverbs, famous quotations from the Bible, very popular song titles—any phrases at all that have become trite through too common usage are sure to make trite titles. You're bound to suspect that a novel will be equally stale in language and plot if the author has given it a title like *Time Will Tell, Murder Will Out, The Worm Turns, An Eye for an Eye, A Scream in the Night,* or *Love Thy Neighbor,* and most of the time you'll be right.

If you're planning to use a biblical or literary quotation or some other familiar phrase as the title of your script, don't do so if it's a recognizable cliché. There are usually only two instances when proverbs and sayings and quotations make good titles: when they're familiar enough to be recognized but not so familiar that they're trite (for example, *The Naked and the Dead*), and when the triteness is canceled out by an amusing or interesting twist.

Robert Benchley, for example, worked quite an amusing book title out of the cliché about the early bird that catches the worm. The proverb itself is ancient and trite enough to be usable only for sewing on samplers: *The Early Bird* would just never do. Instead, Benchley called his book *The Early Worm.* (The angle, of course, is that the proverb may prove the wisdom of early rising because only the bird that rises early gets breakfast—but look what happens to the poor worm that gets up early.) Mystery writers, too, have made quite an art of twisting trite phrases into fresh and interesting titles. To name a few examples: *Let Me Kill You, Sweetheart; The Facts of Death; Dead Ernest; Has Anybody Here Slain Kelly?; Just Around the Coroner; The Quack and the Dead; Grave and a Haircut;* and *Every Little Crook and Nanny.*

The school-composition type of title, such as *A Trip to the City* or *A Month in the Country,* misses because it doesn't offer much promise of excitement. Those scripts sound as though they'll be dull descriptions of the details of that trip or that vacation—(*"We got on the bus and the man stamped our tickets and we saw a lovely bluejay,"* etc.)—in which case they lack problems and all the rest, and, of course, aren't books at all. If, therefore, you're planning to use a title of that sort because the dramatic events *happen* during the trip or during the day in the country, don't do it; you're putting the accent on the wrong syllable. Make your title suggest the interesting aspects of events. A title like *A Sunny Afternoon* is deadly dull, but one like Hemingway's *Death in the Afternoon* is not, because it points to a specific and interesting story line.

You can probably, by now, think of other too general titles that give no real promise of an absorbing plot or that anything interesting will be happening. Here are a few that come to mind: *Day unto Day, Night Falls on Hoboken, Happy Circus Days.*

Titles that are incomprehensible won't do your book much good, either. P. G. Wodehouse, for example, once delivered to me a new manuscript titled *Money for Jam.* The title had to be changed because anyone unfamiliar with British slang, which means the bulk of American readers, would not know that it means money that is easy to get, or money on which you can count. The publishers changed the title to *Money in the Bank,* which is our way of saying the same thing. The same applies to big-word titles: it's difficult to conceive of many readers getting excited over a book entitled *The Dolichocephalic Man,* though *The Long-Headed Man,* which means the same thing, sounds odd enough to be intriguing.

Be careful, too, about titles that are misleading—that sound like one type of book when you're writing another. If, for example, you're doing a college-background novel, in which a hazing occurs and the heroine is locked in a room with a ketchup-stained dummy made to look like a corpse, don't call it *Murder on the Campus.* In the same way, don't make love sound like a Western, just because it takes place on a dude ranch, by calling it *Blazing Guns,* or a murder script (wherein the female corpse is found clutching a bouquet of roses) sound like a love story by calling it *Roses for My Darling.* One famous example occurred when a Raymond Chandler murder mystery was released as a film under the same title as his book: *Farewell, My Lovely.* Apparently the book got by without much trouble because Chandler's byline and other markings identified it as a mystery, but the film version caused so much confusion among moviegoers that the producers had to yank the prints back and retitle the picture *Murder, My Sweet.* The danger of misleading titles is that the readers who like your type of book but think yours is another type may skip it, and readers who like the kind of book yours appears to be, but isn't, may buy it and feel cheated. It isn't absolutely necessary to categorize your book specifically in the title, but do be careful the title doesn't make the book seem to fit into the wrong category.

The same principle applies to the use of humorous titles for serious books and vice versa. You can see that a title like *The Lost Weekend* was perfect for the film and book—it conveys wonderfully the mood of the story—but try on for size a title like *Gimme a Quick One, Bartender.* This is not as extreme an example as you may think, either; editors receive an enormous number of submissions whose titles are exactly opposite to their mood. (I'll never forget the time we received a delicate and tender little story about a mother whose son had been hit by a car and had to have both his upper limbs amputated. The author had titled it *Look, Ma, No Hands.* Now there's an extreme example, but it's true.) Watch this, please: the title should fit the tone as well as the type.

When you select a title, try to choose one that conveys a hint of what the story is about, and of the interesting stuff in the book. Don't, however, give more than a hint: make sure you aren't giving away too much of the plot and theme. A while ago, for example, we received a humorous novel from a client—a novel about the meek wife of a U.S. senator who winds up saving the nation from a nuclear attack. The wife's name is Amanda, so the author called the book *Amanda, Saviour.* The title was certainly interesting enough to catch the attention of the reader, but we felt it was bad because it gave away the solution. We took the book out to market, anyway, and made a deal for it, but, sure enough, the title was changed.

If you're writing a book that builds up to the scene where

a big explosion occurs, don't call your book *The Big Explosion,* no matter how much you like the sound of that title, and no matter how much you may think the readers and the publisher will like it. No title is so good that it must be used even though it will injure the book.

On the other hand, of course, steer clear of the other extreme; titles that are so vague or ambiguous or so faintly connected with the script that the reader can't figure out, after he finished the book, where the title comes in. You've undoubtedly run across a few of those; the titles are interesting enough, but you just can't figure out what they have to do with what you've just read. I've spent years trying to figure out some like that; it's my uneasy suspicion that the writers just got tired of trying to think up good titles and stuck on the first three or four words that came to their minds.

One that I did manage to figure out, after much effort, was a script about a woman who'd promised her late husband that she'd always remain faithful to his memory but became an enthusiastic and nonstop nymphomaniac before his body had cooled. The author called the script *Whirling John,* and you'll understand my puzzlement when I tell you that no character in the story was named John, and nothing or no one in the script did any whirling. It took me a full hour to remember an old joke I'd heard years before.

In the joke, a man named John Smith discovers that he's dying, calls his wife to his bedside, and makes her promise that she'll always remain true to his memory and never have anything to do with another man. She promises, and he dies and goes to heaven, and eventually his best friend dies and goes to heaven, too. The friend wants to look up Smith, and goes to St. Peter for help in finding him. "John Smith, eh?" St. Peter says. "That's a tough one—we have a lot of John Smiths up here. Can you tell me anything else about him?" The friend thinks for a while. "Well," the friend says, "this John Smith told his wife that he'd turn over in his grave if she was ever unfaithful to him."

"Aha!" says St. Peter, his face lighting up. "You mean *whirling* John Smith!"

It's easy to picture the obscurity of this title for anyone who had not heard this joke. We asked the author to change it—as you should if you find yourself about to use an unclear title. The object, to put it in simplest terms, is to select a title that is offbeat enough to be intriguing, but that becomes totally clear and meaningful when the reader has finished the book. Two perfect examples are Norman Mailer's *Tough Guys Don't Dance* and Alice Walker's *The Color Purple*.

Two other types, finally, that are best to avoid: the ultra-arty title (such as *Catch Up the Torch from Faltering Hands*) and the present-tense title (such as *Johnny Brown Saves a Marriage*). You'll still see them around occasionally, but they've become unfashionable and unpopular.

Naturally, the use of a poor title on your script is not the worst thing you can do in the writing business. Editors always have a good supply of blue pencils on hand to change the titles they don't think are right; and besides, there have been hundreds of books published under perfectly awful titles that have done very well. In the early stage of the game, however, when the presence of your byline on a script doesn't yet signal automatically that the book is a good one, little things are sometimes enough to tip the scales against you. That first bad impression made by a poor title may be just enough to give the editor the subconscious nudge into throwing an almost-but-not-quite-right script into the rejection pile; it may be just enough to keep the reader from buying a book by a name unknown to him. It isn't much effort to get a good title instead of settling for a bad one, so you might as well do it right.

20

YOUR WAY WITH WORDS
Style

You've noted, as we've discussed one point after another, that there are many things to worry about in this writing business. Well, the development of your own style is not one of them.

There's only, to misquote Samuel Goldwyn, one thing you have to do to develop an individual style: nothing. Your writing style is like your body—it grows and shapes itself in the normal course of everyday living.

The factors that mold a man's writing style are the same factors that make him want to write. Heredity enters into it, and childhood reading, and adult reading, and the modes of speech and other influences of the people around him throughout his life. All these things affect each writer somewhat differently, and give him a style as definitely his own as his fingerprints.

As a result, you don't ever have to worry about developing a style of your own because, my friend, you've already done so. Inescapably or happily, whichever way you want to look at it, you write the way you write, and I write the way I write, and everybody else writes the way he or she writes.

It is sometimes, or perhaps even usually, rather difficult to realize this fact about your own stuff. You're a little too close to all the trees to see the forest: your own way of thinking is so much a natural part of you, and the words and sentences you use seem such inevitable selections, that it's hard to realize that your own particular personality and background are directing you and causing you to choose words and sentences and language a little or a lot different from anybody else. You're so closely and personally and mentally tied up with the birth of your scripts and with the processes of their manufacture that, though they may look good to you, you'll rarely be able to discern personally the distinguishing trademarks.

Not so an objective reader, however: let him read enough of your stuff so that he's genuinely familiar with it, and he'll be able to spot one of your new scripts at thirty paces, even if it's signed with the byline of Stephen King or Judith Krantz or Genghis Khan. The discovery is usually a little startling to me about my own work, too. I say or write things in the way I do because they seem at the time to be the best way—or at least a reasonable way—to say or write them, and not because I'm making any particular or conscious effort to sound like myself or different from anyone else. But people often write me after the appearance of my articles on technique in the writers' trade magazines, or the appearance of my other stuff elsewhere, and tell me they liked my style or they knew *I* was writing the moment they scanned the page. This information is pleasant to hear, but it's surprising, because, as I say, it's difficult to conceive that you automatically sound a little different from everybody else. In the same way, many of the hundreds of writers my agency represents may believe that their styles are not especially distinctive, yet it's my solemn boast (which I prove regularly) that I can read several unsigned pages of manuscript by any of them and tell at once whose work it is.

Naturally, there are some writers whose works are more heavily stylized than others. Among present-day writers—and writers of all time, for that matter—there are those whose styles pop right out at you the first time you read their stuff, whose styles are so different or unusual that you're always conscious of them. Usually these styles are artificial, deliberately created by the author for their own effect, and sometimes they enhance a book and make it more interesting. More often, however, they have the fault of being so bizarre and attention-grasping that they distract the reader from the story line. And, therefore, most professional writers prefer to use their own natural styles, which are distinctive enough naturally to trade-mark their work, but not so spectacularly different that the reader is continually reminded that he's reading.

You must remember that the primary function of your writing style is communication, the job of communicating the story to the reader in the clearest and most direct way. The differences in natural style result from the differences in language used by each writer to express and communicate the events to the reader, and to make the reader feel the proper emotions as the events are told. When the style goes beyond the purpose of communication—when it's so visible in itself that it takes the reader's attention away from the events—it is usually not doing its job adequately.

There's a newsman's anecdote that seems to me to express very clearly the error of becoming so conscious of your pretty style that you forget that your real job is to tell a story. It concerns a city editor who found himself short-staffed when the Johnstown flood suddenly occurred, and had to send a raw new cub to cover it.

After many hours of nervous waiting, the cub's coverage wire was finally received. It was about five thousand words long, contained practically no facts, and was expressed throughout exactly like its opening sentence: "God sits tonight in judgment at Johnstown."

Curtly, the editor wired back: "Forget the flood; interview God."

Fiction scripts, of course, are rarely the mere bare statements of fact that newspaper stories are. Your style must embellish the facts and round them out and make them interesting and dramatic, though not at the expense of pace and movement.

I believe it was Dickens who said that the thing for an author to do with the outstanding phrases and sentences in his work is strike them out. In moderation, that's good advice. It's a little extreme because I believe no writer in the world can resist sticking in a good phrase or line when he happens to think of one, and besides, occasional outstanding lines spice up the script and don't distract too much. When, however, every stay at the typewriter is a constant struggle to achieve a beautiful style, and when you find yourself leaning over backward to make every sentence a thing of beauty and a joy forever, it's time to realize that you're overdoing it. Just concentrate on telling your story; your good style will take care of itself, without becoming too much of a good thing.

Overwriting of any kind is bad stuff. The effect is always distracting when you use six adjectives where one would do, or when you use too many poetic words *("the man's feral eyes gleamed as he looked at the gibbous moon"),* or when you describe a character's reactions to a situation in such great and exaggerated detail that the effect becomes ludicrous. The current technique regarding the latter, as a matter of fact, is to *underplay* very dramatic scenes.

This term, borrowed from the theater, is the difference between the old-style and the new-style actor's method of depicting emotion. The old-style actor tears at his hair, screams and groans, wrinkles his face into a thousand creases to show grief; an actor like one of the admirable Roberts (Duvall, DeNiro, or Redford) sometimes shows the same thing, and many times more effectively, by standing still and rigid with shock. In a book, the old, overwritten style was used to describe an emotion such as grief by going into great and wordy detail; today authors show the same emotion far more effectively by hinting at it, by suggesting it so delicately that the reader's imagination goes to work and makes him see it all the more clearly.

There is an example of this in the Western about the blind man, previously discussed. To gain sympathy for the blind man's feeling of uselessness, particularly in a setting like the Old West, where physical prowess and physical capabilities were so important, you could easily overwrite the scene by giving the blind man a long, tear-jerking speech about his condition, and how he can't earn a living, and how nobody gives a damn about him, and so on far into the night. The author underplays it with a single line, which is much more effective: *"Us blind fellows ain't kept too busy, Lorna," he said softly.*

It seems to me that there is a hopelessness reflected in that sentence; it seems to me that it sums up a great deal of sadness without a lot of overwriting.

In humorous fiction, Wodehouse was a master at the art of underplaying scenes. Supposing you were describing a discussion between two men, in which one is a tough old bird and the other is badly scared. You can easily overwrite it by giving an overlong description of the frightened man's white face, the perspiration on his palms, the way he runs his finger around his collar. Wodehouse underplays it by merely suggesting it: *He flicked the ash from his cigar. I did not need to do it to mine.*

Again, here is Wodehouse, underplaying in describing a man's reactions at being faced by a hunting rifle: *The fascination of shooting as a sport depends almost wholly on whether you are on the right or wrong end of the gun.*

For an excellent example of underplaying and understatement that greatly increases the effectiveness and emotional strength of a story, I refer you to Stephen Vincent Benét's *Too Early Spring,* particularly the concluding lines.

The lack of rhythm in style—too many short sentences or too many long sentences in a row—is almost always an unnatural state resulting from too much worry over getting the proper mixture. Most people think and talk and write in a natural mixture of short and long sentences; you'll always get it if you forget about it and concentrate on telling your story. This will be a problem only if you make it so.

21

"AND IN THE BEGINNING ..."
The Opening

There are three points at which the normal script, told in chronological fashion, can open: just before the problem comes up, just as the problem comes up, and just after the problem has come up. It's important that you make the correct choice as you settle down to write your book.

Let's take a look at the same book opened in each of the three ways. The just-before-the-problem opening first:

> They stood there silently in the sunlight for a moment, a couple of kids in love, too full of happiness to speak. Then the church bells began to chime in the village, and Joe Benson grinned ruefully.
>
> "I was hoping those bells would never ring," he said, "but there they are. Five o'clock—and I'd better get home and finish up those organizational charts. How would it look if the new general manager of Townsley and Marshall turned up tomorrow for his first day on the job and didn't have his charts ready?"
>
> Della Lane's lovely young face was solemn. "That would never do," she said. "You've got to make them glad they've given you this opportunity—glad they've allowed a newcomer to buy a partnership in the oldest firm in town. You've got to do everything right."
>
> They walked slowly down the road toward Della's home, hand in hand. "You bet," Benson said. "Sure would be sad if I got fired on my first day, after I'd invested every nickel I have in the world. Not that they could, of course."
>
> They reached the gate to the house, and kissed with a sort of desperation born of the knowledge that they'd be apart for all of twenty-four hours. Then Benson jumped into his car and drove back to his own house.

The evening paper lay open on his porch, and the headline story made his heart lurch sickeningly within him. It said the treasurer of Townsley and Marshall had absconded with the company funds, and that the firm had collapsed.

I've telescoped this for space reasons, of course; the scene can actually run considerably longer before the problem shows up.

Here is the same opening just as the problem arrives:

The sound of the morning paper thumping on the front porch awoke Joe Benson, and he tumbled out of bed cheerfully, put on a bathrobe, and went down to get it. Life looked very bright to him, and he whistled as he walked. Just one more day, and he'd begin work as the new general manager at Townsley and Marshall.

And then he opened the paper, and his dreams crumbled into little pieces and dissolved before his eyes. The headline story said that the treasurer for Townsley and Marshall had absconded with the company funds, and the firm had collapsed.

The newspaper dropped from Benson's fingers. He was wiped out—finished. He had put every nickel he owned in the world into buying a partnership in the firm.

He went to the phone to call Della Lane. . . .

Again somewhat telescoped, but the difference is obvious. The other version makes a preliminary build-up before the problem appears; this one shows the problem at once. And here is the same scene as it would be written after the problem has arrived:

Joe Benson sat numbly for a long while, his fingers crumpling and uncrumpling the morning paper. Finally, he got to his feet and, like a man walking in his sleep, went over to the phone and dialed Della Lane's number.

Her sweet young voice held a note of banter. "Joe!" she said. "Why aren't you busy working on the organizational report you promised your new partners?"

His voice surprised even him when he replied: it was harsh and filled with bitterness. "Haven't you seen the morning paper, Della?" he asked.

"Why, no," she said, "not yet, Joe—what's the matter?"

"I'm wiped out," he said. "The treasurer at Townsley and Marshall has absconded with the company funds. The firm's collapsed."

This version, of course, differs from the others because it opens with the problem already on the scene, and with the lead character recovering from his initial shock and about ready to begin action to solve his problem. All three versions, naturally, move through some more building up of the problem—to show why he can't just shoulder his loss and get another job and make more money; to give some reason why it's *urgent* to get his money back—to eventual struggles to solve the problem. The three differ in the degree of rapidity with which the problem is covered and passed and the struggles begun.

All three types of opening are fine, and turn up in equal amounts in published books. The matter of choice depends entirely upon the comparative dramatic strength of the opening events.

If you have an idea for an introductory or pre-problem scene that seems to you to do very well the double job of introducing the lead character interestingly while it emphasizes the gravity or blackness of the subsequent problem (by showing the comparative brightness of things *before* the problem arrived), then the pre-problem opening is the one to use. If the arrival of the problem itself seems to you to be more interesting and dramatic than the events immediately preceding it, or than a description of the lead character's post-problem reactions, then the just-as-the-problem-arrives opening is best. And if a description of the lead character's reactions to the problem, or his first move to solve the problem, strikes you as the more dramatic event in the script you're planning, then by all means start with the just-after-the-problem-has-come-up opening.

There are dangers attached to each of the three: look out for them. If you use the just-before-the-problem type of opening, don't run the pre-problem scene too long. The problem is the thing that really grips and holds the reader and, however interesting the pre-problem scene may be, he won't be willing to wait too long for the trouble to show up.

And if you use the just-as or just-after openings, don't devote so much attention to describing the arrival of the problem or the post-problem action that you forget all about your lead character. Try to build up a picture of him and of the other important characters, as the examples given began to do. Remember that your reader will be interested in the problem only if he's interested in the character who has it.

Whichever type of opening you choose, try to get all the major characters into the script as close to the opening as possible, preferably within the first quarter of the book. The reader wants to know as intimately as possible the people to whom things happen or who are a part of the things that happen, and it's never entirely satisfactory when a new character pops up too late in the script and is the cause or a part of a major plot development.

Don't, of course, go to the other extreme, either—rush so hard to get your major characters into the script early that you get them all in within the first fifty words, and bewilder the reader the way most people in real life are bewildered when they're introduced to a roomful of people all at once. This sort of thing will never do:

> Tom Fowler grinned wryly as he walked into his apartment and almost tripped over a mop and pail. Wasn't that just like Midge, to make such a fuss about keeping things tidy, and then leave everything in the middle of the floor just to run downstairs with Mike and Alice. Well, she'd be back soon, unless she had stopped off afterward to see Eileen, or to have dinner with Slim. And in any case, he had more important things to think about. It was urgent that he phone Sam and Henry and tell them about Arthur, and warn them not to let Jane know about Bob, Max, Charlie, and Gloria.

Introduce your characters early, but not so very close on the heels of one another that they don't emerge as separate entities. Give the reader breathing space between them, and try to establish, as each character appears, or fairly soon afterward, his relationship to the others.

The use of the narrative hook as the start of any type of opening—just-before, just-as, or just-after—achieved an immense amount of popularity years ago and has now simmered down to the point where it's usable only when greatly modified. For those unfamiliar with this phrase, a narrative hook is a startling or shocking first sentence that hooks the reader and pulls him forcibly into the script.

Let us say, for example, that you open your script with this sentence: *Hank Rogers walked over to a dark corner and, stealthily, changed heads.*

That's a narrative hook: it's certainly sufficiently startling so that the reader will read on just to find out what's meant— how a man can possibly change his head. And even when the reader learns that the scene is a masquerade ball, and Rogers has just substituted one papier-mâché head for another, he will, presumably, go on reading.

The narrative hook in its original one-startling-sentence form died a fairly rapid death, or at least sank quickly into severe paralysis, for two reasons: overuse and general crudity. After all, if you see book after book after book with narrative hooks of that type, each shocker trying to outshock all the other shockers, you reach the point where an opening sentence is startling only if it says merely that the day was bright and sunny.

Modified, the narrative hook is still a good idea; anything that pulls the reader into the book is good. A provocative sentence, for example, will often work the trick: *Judy always arrived early at the station so she could get a seat in the first car.*

There's nothing particularly shocking or startling about this—which, for reasons given, is fine—but it *is* interesting. Why, the reader wonders, is it so important that she get a seat in the *first* car—and he reads on.

You're also doing fine when you consider your opening scene or first few scenes as a narrative hook, because, after all, the purpose of the beginning is to hook and interest your reader into reading the rest of the script. You're flirting with triteness and crudity when you employ the narrative hook in its narrowest interpretation, meaning *only* a startling opening and *only* in the first or first few sentences. In its broad interpretation, however—as the fact that your general opening should interest and hook the reader and pull him into the book—it's a good thing to do.

For an excellent example of a narrative hook that occupies an entire chapter of a book, I refer you to the first chapter of a classic mystery novel, *Eight Faces at Three,* by Craig Rice, in which a character moves in puzzlement through a house and finds that every timepiece in every room has stopped at exactly three o'clock. You'll find it difficult to prevent yourself from reading the remaining chapters after you've read this first one.

One other type of opening device that has gone almost entirely out of fashion is the dialogue opening, of which the following is an example:

"Look—there it comes again!"
Ray Latimer shouted these words as he watched the small red airplane buzzing the house down the road.

Overuse has killed this one, too: it was such a standard opener in most books written around the turn of the century that it looks more than a little old-fashioned today. There's also the question of whether you can interest a reader in a line of dialogue when you haven't yet interested the reader in the character speaking the line. Most current readers dislike the device and you'd better let it molder in its grave.

22

QUOTE, END QUOTE
Dialogue

The difference between dialogue in real life and dialogue in fiction is that fiction dialogue must have point and destination. It can never be merely general or polite conversation.

In real life, two men can meet on a street corner and talk for an hour without saying anything of importance to the lives of either of them. In real life, two men can meet for an important conference and spend fifteen minutes in general conversation before they get down to the important items. The funds in real life of how-are-you, how's-the-wife, nice-weather-we're-having, ever-hear-the-one-about, and all the rest are inexhaustible. In fiction, however, every line in the script must move and advance it toward its inevitable destination, and dialogue must do its part.

All fiction, when you stop to consider it, doesn't reflect life exactly as it happens, but instead gives a picture of faster-moving and more directly-moving life by condensing and highlighting. When you plot a book or story, you use a series of events that could conceivably happen in real life (or, if you're doing a fantasy, a series of events that could conceivably happen in real life provided that the basic fantastic concept is accepted), but you're actually condensing and highlighting life by using only events directly related to the situation—and leaving out unrelated events, and all the casual meetings with persons unrelated to the events, and descriptions of all the mechanics of everyday living (three meals a day, toothbrushing, hair combing, etc.). When you're describing a character or locale in a book, you don't describe every detail; you condense and highlight by giving just enough of the important facts to build an accurate picture. And when you use dialogue, you condense and highlight by using only essential and related conversation—conversation that advances the plot directly by adding new information, or indirectly by giving a clearer picture of the characters or their relationships to each other.

Fiction conversation, then, is real-life conversation without its sidetracks or its traditional opening gambits, or at least without most of them. It is the meat, the substance, of real-life conversation, with a little general or unrelated conversation added only when necessary to achieve a more realistic effect.

You've undoubtedly seen a great many loan requests handled this way in fiction:

> There was a knock on the door, and Jerry walked over and opened it. Martin hurried into the room.
> "Jerry," he said, "you've got to help me. They're going to throw me out of my apartment if I don't pay my rent by three o'clock. You've got to let me have two hundred bucks until Thursday."

However urgent the need, few real-life conversations approach the point so directly. In real life, there'll be a knock on the door, and Jerry will walk over and ask who it is, and Martin will answer, and Jerry will say, "Well, for Pete's sake—of all people," and he'll open the door and they'll shake hands. And Jerry will call his wife and say, "Look who's here," and Martin will ask Jerry's wife how she is and ask Jerry how he is, and Jerry's wife and Jerry will ask Martin how he is and how his wife is, and they'll discuss the state of health of their children, and discuss the last time they saw each other and what they've been doing since then, and the conversation will circle around and around a while longer until Martin comes to the request for the money—the only part of the conversation, if it were fiction, in which the reader would really be interested.

The loan-request example, of course, is conversation at top speed to point up Martin's excitement and the urgency of the request. It can also be handled more slowly:

> There was a knock, and Jerry walked over to the door.
> "Yes?" he said. He pulled the door open when the caller replied. "Well, what do you know?" he said. "Martin Sloane!"
> Sloane stepped into the room. "Hello, Jerry," he said. "It's nice to see you again."
> "Nice to see you, too," Jerry said. "What brings you out to this part of town?"
> Sloane hesitated for a moment. "It's this way, Jerry," he said slowly. "I'm in trouble—thought maybe you could help me out. They're going to throw me out of my apartment if I don't pay my rent by three o'clock." His voice quickened, became desperate. "You've got to let me have two hundred bucks until Thursday."

Here the point is reached more slowly, and something of Martin Sloane's natural embarrassment is shown, but this dialogue is still considerably more sped up and condensed than real-life conversation. It sums up this way: much real-life conversation is aimless and pointless, and aimlessness and pointlessness in fiction just won't hold readers. You should no more include unessential and uninteresting dialogue than you should include unnecessary scenes or events that have nothing to do with the plot.

Don't, of course, go to the other extreme and run your conversations like this:

> There was a knock on the door, and Jerry walked over and opened it. Martin hurried into the room.
> "Getting tossed out of my room unless I pay the rent by three —gimme two hundred till Thursday."

You don't have to make your characters talk like telegrams in order to leave out unessentials. Make your conversations as normal-sounding and realistic as possible, but leave out most of the frills usually found in real-life conversations.

Comparatively few scripts sell that contain less than twenty percent dialogue, and unquestionably a goodly amount of dialogue in a book is preferred by readers. You've probably seen people flip through the pages of a book and gauge the amount of dialogue when deciding whether or not to read it, because books with lots of dialogue are usually easier and more pleasant to read than those with long stretches of unbroken narration. Dialogue, however, must never be included for the sole sake of having a lot of it; like all other fiction ingredients, it must do its part to keep the story moving along.

Just as one big chunk of narrative can become boring, incidentally, so can one big chunk of dialogue—a long speech from one person. When a long speech is necessary, try to break it up by inserting dialogue from other persons. You want to avoid, wherever possible, any unbroken stretches in your story— page-long paragraphs of narrative or dialogue. Explanations usually suffer from this fault, and here is how one such speech, which would otherwise run too long unrelieved and without a break, might be broken up:

> Mike turned and looked at Amy.
>
> "You're the killer, Amy," he said. "You hated Rosalie because she stole Joe away from you. You had access to the poison because everybody knows that your hobby is collecting rare old drugs. You went over to her house the night she was leaving for Cincinnati for the weekend, hid in the closet until the place was empty, and then sneaked in and put poison in all her reducing pills. Then you made sure that she'd take a pill soon by asking her when she came back if she didn't think she'd gained a little weight."
>
> Suddenly Amy didn't look sweet and innocent. Her fingers twisted into claws, and she said, "You're out of your mind."
>
> Mike shook his head. "No," he said, "maybe it's just that I'm sane for the first time in months. You were the one who shot Stanley, too, when you felt he was getting too close to the truth. I wondered why you were wearing a coat that warm summer day we met just outside the old barn. You put it on because there were bloodstains all over your blouse . . ." •
>
> Lieutenant Summers cut in nervously. "I hope you can prove all this, Mike."
>
> "Don't worry about it," Mike said. "I can prove everything. I can also prove that when Stanley didn't die from the bullet wounds . . . "

You can see where Mike's explanation would total up to quite a long passage if Amy and Summers had not interrupted. Whenever a character must make a long speech in a script, try to have another character say something every once in a while. If he's talking, he's talking to somebody; have that somebody chip in with a few words at logical moments. Or, if he's making a banquet speech or something of that sort, where you find it difficult to interrupt him with dialogue by another character, have him interrupt himself to take a drink of water, clear his throat, point to someone, etc.

Indirect dialogue, where you tell rather than show the reader what the characters are saying, is usually a bad idea because you're passing up a logical opportunity to get some more "live" dialogue into your story. Here is an example of indirect dialogue:

> He told her that he loved her and that it was silly for them to live apart any longer, and she said that she felt the same way.

This sort of things turns up in new writers' manuscripts quite often, and it isn't wise. For no logical reason, it passes up a legitimate opportunity for dialogue by covering the conversation in a far less dramatic way. Don't do it.

There are three instances in which indirect dialogue should be used. One is where you're running a long stretch of conversation between characters, and feel that a brief pause for indirect dialogue for a few lines will be a refreshing break. Choose, of course, the least important part of the conversation to do that. Another is where a piece of conversation must be recorded in the script, but where the exact conversation is not important or interesting enough to be given in detail. (For example, *"He told him exactly how to operate the new computer."*) And the third is where a piece of action or conversation that has already occurred in the script is later described to another character. (For example, *"He met Joan on the way back from the court-house, and told her about the testimony Sam had given at the trial."*)

Except for these three instances, use direct dialogue in preference to indirect every time. The more "live" dialogue you get into your script, provided it's always relevant, the better.

When you use dialogue, make sure that, aside from the fact that it's condensed, it always sounds natural—the way people really talk. Don't ever, for example, make dialogue unnatural just to convey a fact to the reader. Very often in beginners' stories, one character will say something like this to another character: "I saw your father, John H. Collins, on the street the other day." Obviously, the author's purpose is to tell the reader the father's full name, because it will later be important in the script—but after all, people just don't talk that way. Collins knows his father's full name, and it's doubtful that he has such a variety of fathers that specific identification is necessary. If a fact of this sort is essential to the script, it must be brought out in a more logical and natural fashion; for example:

"I saw your father on the street the other day, Collins," Joe said.
"I haven't had a chance to visit him in months," Collins said. "How did old John H. look? Pretty healthy, I hope."

And remember when you're writing dialogue that people don't talk like printed text or as though they've been rehearsing their lines. I've seen a great many unpublished manuscripts that contain passages like the following:

"I walked over to the window to examine the jewelry display," Frank said. "Going to the side of the window, I saw that the big pendant was missing."

The latter sentence is unnatural because it's what you might call a typical written rather than spoken sentence; people rarely part their sentences in formal ways in normal, unrehearsed speech. Say it aloud and you'll see what I mean: it has too planned and too narrative a tone about it. The natural way to say it would be something like this:

"The stuff in the right showcase was okay, but then I looked at the left showcase, and the big pendant was missing."

It's a good idea, incidentally, particularly when you're starting out in the writing business, to say aloud any bits of dialogue that seem suspect to you. If they sound unnatural or stiff, discard them. When you become more experienced, your mind's ear will begin automatically to reject unsuitable dialogue.

If you worry a lot about thinking up substitutes for "said," make a simple little experiment. Select a half-dozen chapters from current books and make a tally of the amount of times they use "said," and the amount of times they use substitutes. You'll find, perhaps to your surprise, that substitutes are used less than ten percent of the time.

The impression that it's a good idea to use constant substitutes for "said" for variety's sake is incorrect, because there's nothing wrong with "said" itself. The purpose of the word and its myriad substitutes is to identify the person doing the speaking, and there's really no reason to get fancy about it. It's the things that are *being* said that count, not the means of tying the speech to the speaker.

Nearly all the time, the word "said" itself—and its plain and simple alternatives such as "asked," "replied," etc.—will do the job quite adequately; or, if an emotion must be shown and the dialogue doesn't accomplish this completely, a simple descriptive word can be added: "said angrily," "said bitterly," "said coldly." Once in a while, a slightly more colorful word is needed, such as "yelled" or "shouted."

But the constant hunt for substitutes for "said"—the avoidance of this best word and the steady substitution of "reiterated," "observed," "conjectured," "ejaculated," and others of the same type—does far more harm than good. The word that accomplishes speaker identification is supposed to do so in a quiet and unobtrusive manner. Constant variation and use of big words fail in their purpose because they become distractions in themselves.

Another thing that should not be done is the trick of splitting up dialogue in unusual manners. Here's a sentence in the normal manner:

> "I'm going to take you home," Jim said.

Here is the sentence split up in an unusual manner:

> "I'm going," Jim said, "to take you home."

Or even, in its more consciously cute version:

> "I'm going to take," Jim said, "you home."

The unusual split in dialogue enjoyed a brief flurry of popularity but, like all artificial devices, it was quickly overused and its popularity has now almost completely ended. When you write the sections of dialogue in your scripts, you'll note places at which the "he said"s obviously belong. Be smart: put them there.

In writing long stretches of conversation between two characters, by the way, it's all right to leave out identifying phrases for short stretches because the reader can figure out when character A is talking and when character B is talking by the order of their remarks. Get in your "A said" and "B said" every once in a while, however, or your reader may become confused and wonder why the villain's suddenly saying, "Don't you dare kiss me, you nerd," and the heroine's answering, "Scream all you want—no one can hear you."

One mechanical point: when a stretch of dialogue by a single character is a long one and occupies more than one paragraph, leave out the quotation marks at the end of all paragraphs except the last one. That will identify the whole section as his speech. Here's an example:

> "Well," said Joe, "this thing happened to me when I was just a kid. I decided to skip school one day, and went to the

movies instead. It was there that I met Maisie.

"Maisie was skipping school, too—she was a senior at the Haven for Delinquent Girls—and I fell for her immediately. Maybe it was the obvious purity of her soul, and maybe it was her big—well, let it go. Anyhow, we saw each other every night after that.

"After we'd been going together for a few months . . ."

It's best, as I've said, to interrupt long speeches with dialogue by other characters, but that's the way to do it if you can't manage to work in interruptions.

Most editors today don't like dialect. They feel that it often offends readers of the same race or country of origin because it can sound derisive or satirical, and that it's usually hard to follow and therefore disliked by most readers.

It's about ninety-five percent impossible to sell a script told mostly or entirely in dialect, and your best bet is to avoid dialect altogether. If you *must* use a dialect-speaking character, avoid showing dialect through misspelled words (for example, "Yess, ve haff got goot fresh cake today") and do it through the easier-to-read method of using correctly spelled words plus the occasional addition of a few familiar words in the foreign tongue (for example, "Ja, we have fresh strudel today."). That will often do the trick, and you'll have a much better chance of securing the editorial okay.

23

OVER THE RIVER AND THROUGH THE WOODS
Transition

This is going to be one of the shortest chapters in the book, because the technique of transition is simplicity itself. It's an important subject because a great many writers do it wrong, but you'll have no trouble with it once you understand the simple principles.

Transition is the act of changing from one scene to another, or moving your characters from one place or time to another. Let's cut in at the tail end of a scene and have a look at transition done badly:

> "Don't be an idiot, O'Leary," Keller said. "I must have those plans today."
>
> "And I'll tell you once again that I'm sorry," O'Leary said. "I have strict orders to give the plans to no one but General Masters."
>
> "Will five thousand dollars make you forget your orders? It isn't as though you'll be doing anything illegal. . . ."
>
> "You won't get these plans for five million dollars." O'Leary turned his back and looked down at his desk.
>
> Keller stood there impotently for a moment. Then he shrugged and walked out of the door.
>
> He walked down the corridor to the elevator, waited until it arrived, entered, and rode down the ten floors to the street level. He walked out of the building, went down to the corner to wait for a bus, boarded one, and rode the mile and a half to the center of town.
>
> He got off in front of Police Headquarters, a squat and square red-brick building, and hurried up the stairs to the main entrance. He confronted the sergeant at the desk.

"I'd like to see the chief of detectives," he said.

He had to tell the entire story to the sergeant, and then again to several other officers. Finally, after almost a half hour, he was ushered in to see Chief of Detectives Charles Arlen.

"I want to swear out a warrant for Terence O'Leary of State University," Keller said. "He's stolen some important papers from me. . . ."

The error in this sequence is the transition section: the detailed description of Keller's movements between the end of one scene (when Keller walks out of O'Leary's office) and the beginning of the next scene (which actually starts with the first piece of important action—Keller's talk with Arlen). The reader's interest lies in the scenes in which things occur that are vital to the plot; he neither requires nor is interested in step-by-step accounts of the movement between these scenes.

Here's how the transition should be handled to eliminate the unimportant and dull details of the movements between scenes:

"You won't get these plans for five million dollars." O'Leary turned his back and looked down at his desk.

Keller stood there impotently for a moment. Then he turned and walked out of the room.

A half hour later, Keller sat in front of a wide scarred desk and faced Chief of Detectives Charles Arlen.

"You want to make a formal complaint against this man O'Leary?" Arlen asked.

"You bet I do," Keller said. "He stole my papers, and I want him arrested and the papers returned to me today."

The moment a scene has ended, which means the moment the last piece of important action in the scene has been shown, it's the author's job to close the scene as quickly as possible, and move as quickly as possible to the important action in the next scene. The details of transition do nothing for the script but slow it up and create an unnecessary pause between important action. It's wise to avoid these pauses by closing a scene the moment the last piece of important action has been shown, skipping four single spaces to denote a change of scene or passage of time, and starting right up with the first important piece of action in the new scene. The four-space skip is the automatic sign today that the scene is changing: once asterisks (***) used to do the job, but they're now considered antique.

When it's possible to change scenes with a movement description of one line or so—for example, "He walked across the street and stopped in at the lingerie store to see Diana"—it's all right to do that instead of the four-space skip. It's when the details of transition take too long, boringly long, that they're bad. Your reader rarely has to be told that the character has driven or taken a bus to his next destination, and other such routine things; he'll assume that the character used the normal means of transportation and didn't flap his arms and fly through the air.

Sometimes transition to a new scene can be made even smoother by closing the old one with a hint or statement about the character's next stop. The example given might do that in this way:

> "You won't get these plans for five million dollars." O'Leary turned his back and looked down at his desk.
> Keller stood there impotently for a moment. "All right," he said finally. "Then I'll get the plans another way. I'll tell the police that you stole them from me."
>
> Chief of Detectives Charles Arlen handed Keller a ballpoint pen and a printed form.
> "Sign this complaint at the bottom, please," he said. "We'll issue a warrant and pick up O'Leary."

Here's another example that names both the time and the place of the next scene:

Armstrong put on his coat. "That seems to do it for today," he said. "Don't forget to meet me at the Lakeside Inn tomorrow at nine."

"I'll be there," Jim said.

Jim arrived at the inn right on time, but Armstrong was nowhere around.

Simple enough, you'll agree.

24

STUFFING
THE HOLLOW MAN
Characterization

My dictionary defines character as the sum total of all the qualities that distinguish a person from others. Characterization in fiction, then, to follow this lead, is the method of distinguishing your characters from one another—and thereby enabling your reader to know and understand them better and see them more clearly—by revealing their individual and distinctive qualities or "nature."

It's no longer acceptable to characterize a person, to distinguish him from all the others in the script, by tacking a simple label on him—in other words, by coming right out and calling him greedy, or mean, or good-hearted, or bad-tempered, or dishonest, or anything of that sort. That was all right in more innocent times, when, as we've discussed, readers were apparently more trusting, but it's not all right now. Today's readers all seem to come, at least in spirit, from Missouri: they want to be shown. They're unwilling to accept the author's unsupported word for the nature of the characters: they want to be shown the inner workings of each of them and be allowed to draw their own conclusions.

The means of demonstrating the qualities and makeup of the people in your scripts are exactly the same as the means by which the personalities of real-life people are demonstrated to you in everyday living. How, after all, are you able to gauge and evaluate the inner workings of people around you, and eventually understand them and know them for what they are? You do so through your observation of three types of outward signs: the things they do, the way they act when things happen to them, and their reasons for doing things. To put it another way, you judge people by their actions, reactions, and motivations.

Let's say, for example, that you're walking down the street with an acquaintance, and he stops to buy a magazine at a corner stand operated by a shabby old blind man, counts his change, and hurries you away, and then shows you, at a safe distance, that he's been given an extra quarter by mistake. You don't have to look for a sign on his back, or get an X-ray, to become aware that he's mean and without pity; his action in not returning the coin to the old blind man has shown you that.

Or, if I may address the ladies for a moment, let's say that you're being visited by a man, and a large mouse suddenly runs around the room. You look around, expecting the man to chase the mouse away, and there he is, standing on the coffee table, with his trousers pulled up above his knees. You don't need his horoscope to show you that he's cowardly; his reactions to the mouse have told you that.

And if a man comes to you and tells you a story about the dubious morals of a mutual acquaintance, and you know the story to be absolutely untrue, and realize that it's being told only because the speaker resents the mutual acquaintance's success and hopes to injure him, you know at once that the speaker is an extremely jealous type. You've been made aware of it by his obvious motivation.

Sometimes, as in the examples given, you're able to determine a person's character, or a strong phase of his character, on the basis of a single occurrence; sometimes a lot of things must occur before you can add them up and know him for what he is. However rapidly or slowly you reach your conclusion, it always comes, since you're not a mind reader, from one or a combination of the three outward signs—actions, reactions, motivations.

I believe you can easily see, from the examples given and from others in real life that will occur to you, why the newer method of characterizing by showing the reader is so much better and more satisfying than the old one of just telling him. When someone characterizes another person—tells you the other person is a great guy or a louse, or a coward or exceptionally brave, and so on—you may believe him or you may not; most of the time, if you're a person of good sense and fairness, you'll reserve judgment until you are able to observe the man and form your own opinion. When, however, you see that person in action and form an opinion yourself, you know that the opinion is altogether correct (at least as far as you're concerned) because you've seen for yourself. The show-the-reader method of characterization allows the reader to see for himself and be convinced.

It's not necessary to characterize all the people, major and minor in your stories. Who cares if the man who delivers flowers to the heroine on page 67 and never turns up in the story again is a greedy little creep and complains about his tip and asks for more? Who cares if the cop from whom the lead asks directions on page 109 is a bad-tempered fat man who gives the information grudgingly? You *may* give some of your minor people quick little characterizations if you want to add occasional humorous or realistic touches, but the point is that it's not essential that you do so all or even most of the time: the minor characters play so unimportant a part in the scripts, and appear in the script so briefly, that it isn't necessary for the reader to know and understand them and see them clearly. Some editors, as a matter of fact, feel so strongly about the subject of unimportance of minor characters that they even get revisions of otherwise satisfactory scripts in which too much space and attention is given to characterization and physical descriptions of minor story people. They feel that too heavy focus on the unimportant people, while they're on stage performing their unimportant action, is an unnecessary distraction from the straight story line, and creates further distraction because the reader assumes they're important characters (in view of the amount of attention given them during their appearances onstage) and keeps wondering why they don't come back into the book.

It's vital, however, that all of your major story people be characterized. They must never be a collection of wax figures, all apparently stamped out of the same mold; they must be distinctly different people with distinctly different personalities so that the reader can form distinct pictures and opinions of each of them.

That doesn't mean that you must necessarily differentiate between them by giving them such odd or outstanding characteristics that the dramatis personae of your scripts behave like the membership of the local mental institution. You can, without question, think of four or five young men in your town who are of the same general background—all likeable, all of approximately the same cultural and educational level, and no thieves, abnormally jealous individuals, or cowards among them—and yet each one's personality is obviously and recognizably distinct and different from all the others'. The answer lies in their manner or style, and in their exact approach and attitude toward everything—the sum total of the *smaller* differences in their general actions, reactions, and motivations.

Two of the men, for example, may like the same girl—and, though they may be of the same type generally, their approach to the girl will immediately make them distinguishable. One, a quiet type, would take the girl out often, and try to be pleasant and interesting to her, but would not try to overwhelm her in any way. The other, a more sophisticated and faster-moving type, would send her oceans of perfume, bales of roses, and otherwise try to swamp her into succumbing rapidly.

As characterization in a script, this sort of difference of approach and manner does the job very nicely—for, though neither man possesses extreme characteristics like excessive meanness or cowardice, it's certainly easy to distinguish between them. And when you add the other factors that might mark the difference between an extroverted man and a quiet man—difference in dress (quiet man dresses conservatively; extroverted man dresses with more flash), difference in manner of speech (extroverted man talks rapidly, steadily, confidently; quiet man chooses his words and doesn't say much), difference in social skill (extrovert is comfortable at discos; quiet man is awkward on the dance floor), and so on—you've done a thorough job of characterization on both of them.

In short, the success of your characterizations depends upon the ease with which your readers can distinguish between your characters and recognize their separate personalities. Whether you give them extreme characteristics (for example, one cowardly and one very brave), or whether you make them similar in type but opposite in manner, the important thing is that you make them distinguishable from one another.

You begin to characterize the moment you form the broad outlines of your plot, because you're assigning your characters to roles that will require different actions, reactions, and motivations from each of them. These basic assignments are your start in the job of characterization; the characters' reasons for wanting to solve the problem or (in the case of the opposition) for keeping it from being solved, and their general moves to achieve their purpose, will begin to show generally what kind of people they are. But don't stop there: the characterizations will be complete only if you follow them through into all the specific details of the plot as well.

It's possible, for example, for you to have a character act with logical motivation and right in line with his "side" in the script—that is, heroically or villainously, sympathetically or unsympathetically—and still miss an excellent opportunity for some more characterization. Let's say, for example, that you want to characterize a villain as generally tricky and underhanded in his tactics; yet you write a scene in which the hero goes to an auction to bid on a house he needs desperately, and the villain outbids him and gets the house. The villain's actions are perfectly logical, and properly dastardly, but there's nothing tricky or underhanded about them. You'd add another milestone in your job of characterizing the villain as tricky and underhanded if he had gotten the house in a crooked manner

—perhaps by bribing the auctioneer to overlook the hero's upraised hand.

It's not a requirement for a character to reveal his attitudes and personality in every action he makes. We've already discussed the error of making your characters unbelievably all black or all white, and it will usually do the trick if the villain is shown as more often villainous than good, and the hero as more often good than bad. On the other hand, characterization becomes more pronounced through continued revelation of a specific quality or type of action, and good opportunities to show it are sometimes hard to come by. If one presents itself, it is best to seize it and make full use of it.

I've mentioned one of the opportunities for characterization in different types of clothing; there are many others. A girl who wears too much makeup, no brassiere, and a dress that is several sizes too tight and features an extremely low-cut neckline is characterized almost immediately; there may be exceptions to the rule, but it's doubtful that her favorite sport is singing at church socials. A girl with no makeup, thick glasses, and an unfashionable hairdo is characterized in the other direction. Use this sort of thing when you can.

You'll also help differentiate between your characters by differentiating their physical descriptions in general. Try to avoid having two fat little men in the same script, or two thin young men with horn-rimmed glasses, or two dark-haired young ladies with pixie haircuts, or two men with big mustaches.

The same, of course, applies to your choice of names for your characters. If you have a character named Robertson, don't call another one Williamson. Avoid Jack and Jake, and Larry and Barry. That should be the case even with twins, unless they almost always appear together in the script and their separate actions have no importance. In general, try to avoid two names that sound alike, begin or end alike or similarly, or begin with the same initial.

The character tag is another device that is pretty dead

today because of overuse. This is the stunt where a man or woman is characterized and recognized by constant repetition of the same act, such as flipping a half dollar into the air, or the same phrase or type of phrase, such as "Bless my soul!" It's still possible, I suppose, to think up a fresh character tag, but restrain yourself from using it so often in the script that it becomes irritating as well as characterizing; you'd be much better off skipping this trick entirely. Except in books about long-established series characters, where the public has learned to sigh and take it, most editors react to character tags today by murmuring, "Bless my *soul!*" flipping a rejection slip into the air, and then attaching it to the manuscript.

25

AND THEY LIVED HAPPILY EVER AFTER
The Ending

Just as there are three points at which a novel can be opened, there are also three points at which it can be closed. These points are just before the solution is reached, just as the solution is reached, and just after the solution is reached.

Here is an example of the just-before-the-solution ending:

> He was sure now, and his footsteps quickened as the house came into sight. It had never been Linda, never at all; it had always been Susan. What an idiot a man can make of himself!
>
> Maybe it was too late now ... but at least there was hope. Susan had always understood him, even when he'd been too stubborn to understand himself. Maybe she would understand that this was just another of his mistakes, though by far the biggest one. At least, he knew, it would be his last.
>
> The house looked just the same, and the sight of it up close was a wonderful thing. He straightened his shoulders a little, and put his key in the door.

In the strictest sense, the just-before ending doesn't really happen just before the solution: it happens just before the *full* solution. As in the example given, the main problem is usually resolved, but the question of whether or not the lead character will achieve full happiness is left unanswered, with hope visible but not certainty. In this script the lead character has solved his problem because he's made the correct choice between Linda, a girl with whom he'd become involved, and his wife, Susan, but the full solution is not shown because it's not absolutely certain as the book closes whether or not Susan will take him back.

The just-before ending, of course, occurs in the unresolved script. It's a perfectly acceptable way to conclude a book when the nature of the events seems to demand that sort of ending, but it might be a good idea to keep in mind, as I've said, that "unresolved" is usually a misnomer, and "not fully resolved" is really meant. The reader will feel cheated after the big problem build-up if, at the conclusion, a solution is not at least hinted at or promised—even if the solution is only the fact that the problem is unbeatable.

In the example given, no full solution is shown because that is as it should be. Despite the reader's sympathy for the lead character, he knows that the lead has come very close to making an immensely serious blunder, and he doesn't *want* the lead to be forgiven too quickly or easily. He's pretty sure, however, from the indications in the final paragraphs, that Susan *will eventually* take the lead character back, and so he's satisfied.

Here is an example of the just-as-the-solution ending:

> McCoy nodded to the police officers. "All right," he said, "he's admitted it. I'll see you down at the Hall later on."
> He turned and smiled at Ellen. "We'd better have that dinner right now," he said. "I'm going to be pretty busy in my first few weeks as the new district attorney."

The just-as ending gives the solution in all its details, then cuts right off. It does so smoothly, of course, with a concluding sentence or paragraph such as the one in this example, but the solution scene is always the last one.

And here is an example of the just-after-the-solution ending. It comes from a book in which a sort of running gag has been made of the father's frequent complaints to his son for leaving roller skates on the floor. Later on, however, the son is seriously injured in a school fire, and this is the way the book ends:

> Joe replaced the telephone on its stand, and looked at his wife. Her eyes were wide and frightened, and he took both of her hands gently in his.

"It's all right, Alice," he said. "It's all right. The Doc says I got him to the hospital in time. He says Lonny will be out of there and okay in just a few weeks. . . ."

His grip tightened on his wife's hands. "I'm okay now, too, Alice," he said. "You'll never have to worry about my running away from trouble again."

They stood there in silence for a moment, and then Joe let her go. "I've got to tell Tom!" he said. "He's probably sitting there in his house chewing his fingernails. I won't phone him—I'll run over there. . . ."

He kissed her, and hurried out of the room and along the corridor to the stairs. He had just reached the stairs when his foot caught in a roller skate on the floor, and he slid to the edge of the top stair. He didn't quite manage to grab the railing.

He thumped and bumped down the stairs and, the roller skate still clinging to his shoe, began to slide again—along the bottom floor and out the open door. He hit the sidewalk with a thud which shook the nearby trees.

He sat there, stunned, for a little while, and then got gingerly to his feet and rubbed himself. He stooped, picked up the roller skate, and grinned. When he looked up again, his next-door neighbor was standing nearby and staring at him.

He returned the stare. "Well, what do *you* want?" he asked. "What's wrong with leaving roller skates on the floor? How else can a guy get any exercise around this place?"

The final scene in the just-after ending is, of course, an anticlimax. The important action really ends when Joe tells his wife that their son will be okay and also reveals that *he* is now going to be okay (for the problem of the book is his weakness of character and habit of always running away from trouble instead of facing it squarely). The roller skate scene is not vital to the plot by any means.

Generally, anticlimaxes are bad stuff. The reader is built up all through the script to wait for the solution, and therefore, once that solution arrives he's satisfied. The just-after ending, however, makes the anticlimactic scene satisfactory because it's a relatively short anticlimax, and because it's had so much heralding throughout the script (in this case, all the earlier scenes about the skates) that it becomes a sort of nice extra touch—icing on the cake rather than excess baggage. The roller skate scene is not uninteresting; it's very brief and, in addition to bringing the running gag to an amusing conclusion, it integrates very well with the solution scene because it's a further manifestation of the father's relief over his son's salvation and his own. And in a long novel, there may be several loose ends that you'll want to tie together after the solution has been reached. If the reader has been absorbed in your book all the way through, the chances are he'll stick around for a few closing scenes, as long as you keep them brief and relevant to the plot.

Avoid anticlimaxes that have not been given earlier heralding in the story, which are not the fitting conclusion to earlier material. And avoid *any* anticlimaxes that are too long: that run into too many scenes after the solution has been reached, or that relate the characters' histories too far into the future. (The fairy-tale or down-through-the-third-generation anticlimax is in the to-be-avoided category: *And they always lived happily after that, and had fine children, and, later on, fine grandchildren.* The reader is interested in the solution of the problems, not in the hero's subsequent career as a grandparent.)

If you have a sufficiently strong problem and solution, long anticlimactic details are usually unnecessary, because the solution will generally tell the reader all he has to know—and he can imagine or predict the lead's future. If long explanations are necessary, it's best to get them right into the solution scene before the final and closing piece of important action; in a mystery novel, for example, all the details that lead to the discovery of the killer should be related *before* the killer jumps on the hero and is subdued and led away by the gendarmes. But if you've planted a running gag that leads right to an inevitable added touch, and can keep that anticlimactic scene short, it will do no harm.

It doesn't, incidentally, always have to be a running gag in the humorous sense; it can also be a sequence of serious little events that lead to a satisfying finish: for example, a cowardly lead character always gets pushed around by a big tough guy, and then, after he's overcome his cowardice in some other way in the solution scene, goes back and beats hell out of the tough guy. This was done very effectively in one of the Superman films in which Superman loses his powers and gets roughed up by a unlovable, muscular character in a little restaurant; but then, of course, Superman returns to the restaurant and takes care of the unpleasant character, and it wasn't just kids who shouted their approval of that revenge scene. In fact, if your hero or heroine is humiliated or otherwise mistreated, it's almost mandatory that you have a final scene in which your lead gets back at the person who did the bad stuff earlier in the book. Sometimes writers will fail to do this, either because of forgetfulness or because they fear the getting even scene would be too anticlimactic, and the reader often feels unfulfilled or disappointed.

Use the just-before ending in scripts where the full solution will obviously take a long time and a lot of slow mending—such as the example given. Use the just-as ending when the solution ties up everything extremely satisfactorily and an extra added attraction is neither desired nor needed. And use the just-after ending as discussed.

The punch-line ending has received a great deal of attention. It's the opposite-pole brother of the narrative hook: just as the narrative hook in its basic form tries to pull the reader into the script with an outstanding first sentence or paragraph or two, the punch line tries to send him off smiling happily or dreamily or feeling otherwise satisfied with an outstanding final touch.

An excellent example of the punch line at its best occurs in the stage version of the classic play *Arsenic and Old Lace*. In this play, for those who haven't seen or read it, the hero is distressed by the fact that all the other members of his family are homicidal lunatics, and, as a result, he tries to avoid the heroine because she has marital ideas. At the end, however, he learns that he's not a member of the family at all, but actually the illegitimate son of a servant, and he rushes up to the heroine and takes her in his arms.

"Darling," he tells her happily. "I'm a *bastard!*"

Like the narrative hook, the punch line has been so much overused that good examples today are extremely rare. If you think of the punch line, therefore, only as the very last line of your book, you may easily go awry. Just try to make the entire concluding section of your book satisfying and pleasing to your reader, and you'll do fine.

PART FOUR

THE FINISHED-PRODUCT FACTS

26

THE SLICE AND THE SLASH
Revision

The best way to feel about revision is that you want to do as little as possible of it in the course of your career.

Some writers believe that the only way to create a superior script is to write it and then revise it very extensively, cutting and altering and rewriting words, phrases, sentences, paragraphs, and even entire scenes. Their idea is that a book must be polished, re-polished, and then polished some more in order to make it fully right. It's a common enough theory, but I think that most writers who actually do create superior scripts will agree that it's incorrect.

I've already mentioned the primary danger in planning to do extensive revisions on your scripts: the fact that the subconscious realization that there *will* be further revisions tends to create carelessness in the writing of the first draft (less and less care in the choice of language and phrasing, less and less effort for clarity and the right dramatic effect the first time), with the result that the first drafts become worse and worse, and the revisions heavier and heavier, until the author has almost lost altogether his ability to write clearly and well. You become too dependent, in other words, on the cop-out that you'll fix it up later.

There are, of course, other dangers. One is the fact that however sophisticated you may become about writing as you remain in the business, or however new you may be at the game now, you'll still write your first draft most of the time "in emotional heat." To put it in a different way, it's a fact that, however rapidly your fingers streak across the keys of your word processor or however ploddingly you write your words and sentences with a blunt pencil, you'll still feel the emotional impact of the events most strongly when you first write them, and will pass on that feeling most freshly and vividly in the first draft. When, however, you do many subsequent drafts, you're no longer writing emotionally and freshly; you're going over the same stuff again and again and again and doing the routine job of fixing and patching up. You may improve the wording here and there, and substitute better-phrased paragraphs and sections here and there, but because the emotional drive is gone and you're working and thinking routinely, you'll often polish out the freshness and emotional tone while you're doing it.

Furthermore, there's a saturation point in excessive revision, which is not too hard to reach. As you continue to revise and revise and go over the same ground again and again, you'll eventually become so familiar with the exact phrasing and movement of the script that you'll lose your perspective: you'll become so close to the script and so imbued with it that you'll no longer be able to tell accurately which things are right and which are not so good. And it's a sad thing to contemplate the death blow you can deal a script when you've reached that point but still think you're revising intelligently.

Another objection to excessive revision, particularly since it so often does more harm than good, is that it takes so much time away from *new* work—you're patching up and patching up (and possibly ruining) one script when you could be spending the time writing another. And one last objection is that as you become an established professional, circumstances may arise where you won't be able to do heavy revising—for example, where you're given an excellent and lucrative assignment to write a book on a very short deadline, or where you're given an adequate deadline but things like family problems prevent you from beginning work until relatively close to the agreed delivery date. If you're physically or mentally unable to turn out a first or second draft that is good, you're in trouble.

In general, the best practice is the one indicated at the start of this chapter: try to revise as little as possible by revising only when absolutely necessary. If you can't manage a first-and-final draft, go ahead and do a second draft—but train yourself to write so tightly and carefully that only a limited number of minor revisions of the first draft are necessary before you've got a script that you can take to market. When you finish your draft, it's certainly wise to go over it with a blue pencil and an eagle eye, but make changes only where they're definitely and indisputably necessary—where a word or phrase or section is positively wrong in meaning, or where a word or phrase or section positively does not give the dramatic effect it must give, or something of that sort. Be honest with yourself, and when you're about to alter something for no stronger reason than a whim, or make a substitution that really isn't much better than the original, leave the script alone.

Your initial choice of words and material, made during the emotional drive of creation and in context with the surrounding sentences and the mood of the book, will usually be best, anyhow. You'll find that as you develop the habit of tight writing, revising only where really necessary, your scripts will grow better and the sections that require revision will show up less and less often.

You'll probably also hear, now and then, of the "cooler" or refrigerator method of revision—wherein the writer puts a script away in a drawer the moment he's completed the initial draft, and takes it out and revises it a month or two later, when he's cooled off about the script and can be completely objective in his examination. I've known a great many authors who have tried the refrigerator system, but know almost none who've found it to be of any real value, or whose scripts haven't been done more harm than good by it. The trouble with the method is that, just as too constant association with a book during revision after revision puts the writer too close to it to see and feel it clearly, too long dissociation puts him too far away from it to see and feel it clearly. The author can never become *entirely* objective about his script—as, for example, an editor seeing it for the first time would be—because he retains memories of the processes of writing it and of the emotional mood at that time. But if he takes himself far away from the script and out of its mood, as occurs due to the passage of time while the script is in the refrigerator, it's difficult, when he returns to it once more after the cooling-off period, to get "inside" it again and *feel* where the dramatic effects are inadequate.

It's best, all in all, to attack your necessary revisions when you've just finished your first draft and retain some of the heat and emotional drive of creation; and, by doing so, also get the script completely off your work schedule and your mind so you can be ready for your next job.

Sometimes, of course, you'll pronounce a script completely okay just as it comes out of the typewriter or word processor or after you've made some revisions, and send it off to market—and then learn that some additional revisions are necessary. This occurs when an editor sees or thinks he sees flaws or areas for improvement in your script and indicates that his firm will publish it if necessary repairs are made. Let's look at when to do the revision, and how.

First of all, *don't* rush to your blue pencil and begin to revise a script just because an editor has returned it with a comment such as "too slight" or "too little action." A comment of that sort usually means that the editor thinks your script considerably above the average of those he's read recently, and feels you show promise and he'd like to see more from you, but it's by no means a commitment or even an indication that he'll buy the present script if you eliminate or improve the factors about which he's commented.

You must remember that the editor is not in his job to serve as a one-man criticism bureau. He knows there's something basically wrong with your script that makes it necessary that he reject rather than contract for it, and he jots down a quick comment to guide you on future submissions and to express his interest, but he generally has neither the time nor the inclination to give you a full analysis. The point about which he's commented may not even be the thing that's really wrong with the book, because an experienced editor knows a script isn't right, often without quite knowing why, the moment he reads it, and his comment is a quick guess as to the reason; but a careful, lengthy, thought-out analysis on his part might reveal that the reason was something else again. Or, it may not be the only problem with your book or it may only be the most immediately visible of a number of problems.

In most cases, you'll only irritate the editor when you interpret his friendly comment as a suggestion for revision, alter the script, and send it back to him. Your best bet, when you get a comment of that sort, is to note it as an expression of interest and keep the editor in mind for when you market your next script.

A critical comment from an editor is also not necessarily an indication that revising the script and eliminating the stated objections will make it right for other houses, either. Much of the time, the editor's comment will relate only to the needs of his own list, to the kinds of books published by his particular firm. The script that he criticizes as having too little sex, for example, will often be just right for the next house you try, whose editors don't like too much sexual content in the books they publish. When a number of editors make the same comment, however, it's of course time to take the script off in a corner and see what all the objecting is about.

It's another matter again, naturally, when an editor writes you a detailed letter stating that he likes your script very much but is returning it because of some specific objection, and either says specifically or hints strongly that he'll buy if you can get rid of the problem or problems. If you can think of a way to rewrite the script and eliminate the objections in a manner that will be logical and won't otherwise injure the novel and make it unacceptable for another reason, you should certainly do so. But first write the editor, thank him for his letter, and outline your idea, asking him if he believes the script will be acceptable if you eliminate the objection in that way. If he says "Yes" or "Maybe," get to work.

Most of the time, however, an editor who wants a rewrite will return your script together with a specific request that you do one (or will write and ask that you work from your copy of your script and send him the revised versions of the problem sections), and he'll give you general details on how he wants you to go about it. That usually won't constitute a definite commitment, either, because few editors will make a commitment on an imperfect script unless they know your stuff and are sure that you can make it perfect, but you'll almost always get a contract if you fix as requested. When you begin your revision, you won't have much trouble getting back "into" the script, as in the refrigerator situation, however cold the script may have grown, because there's no situation here of puzzling out which things to revise, and how to do so. Just follow the editor's directions closely.

Don't, by the way, become revision happy in the process, and change six or seven other things while you're fixing the ones the editor has requested. You may alter the very things he likes about your script. And if the revision is a fairly extensive one, don't just cross out words and lines and write or type above them. Redo all the revised pages.

Once in a great while, an editor will make a request for a revision and you'll look over the script and see that he'd missed the point and that the revision is actually unnecessary. He will, for example, say that it's never explained how the hero escapes from the ropes that bind him while he's a captive in the old deserted factory owned by the villain, and yet, on page 219, you have a paragraph that tells how the hero tips over a jar of acid and burns off the ropes and gets loose.

When that sort of thing happens, you will know, more than ever before in your life, the sensation of an irresistible urge. The desire to write the editor and tell him he's a moron will be so strong that you may have to lock yourself up in a closet for a few hours until you get over it. If necessary, lock yourself in the closet—but don't, whatever you do, write and tell him he's a moron.

He can have two kinds of answers to such a letter from you. If he's in a good mood, or if he's a nice person, he'll reply and point out that if he missed it, so may a great many other readers, and you'd better go into more detail in that scene and make it more visible; or he may smile and ask you to return the script intact so that he can reread it and present it to his editorial board. On the other hand, your script may suddenly reappear under your postman's arm.

So if you see that the editor has missed the point, just go ahead—without bothering him—and build it up in greater detail and make it more visible. When you get your check for your advance, you have my permission to smile quietly to yourself as you deposit it in your money market account.

27

MARKETING AND AGENTS
Where to Go with the Completed Script

When you've finished plotting and writing and revising your scripts, you'll want to know how to go about selling them. There are, of course, two methods: submitting them directly to the publishing houses, and submitting them to the publishing houses through a reliable literary agent.

Let's have a look, first of all, at the literary agent situation. I covered the subject of literary agencies pretty thoroughly in an article called "Can We Still Be Friends?" which was published in the trade journal *Writer's Digest**, and quote largely from this article in the material on agents that follows.

A few feet from my desk, off in a dark corner, there's a curious spot on the wall that looks scarred and lacerated and about to cave in. As a matter of fact, it *is* about to cave in—for it has received harsh treatment through the years. It's the section of the wall against which I beat my head.

Most of my clients and potential clients, I'm happy to report, are awfully nice. We exchange lovingly cordial letters when I get them better deals than they expected, and icily cordial ones when I have to confess that I argued for more money with an editor for two hours and he won—and when they come to New York, sometimes I buy them Scotches or martinis, and sometimes they buy Dubonnets with a twist for me.

*Reprinted by permission. The author expresses thanks to the publisher and editor of *Writer's Digest* for permission to reprint his article.

Sometimes, however, some of their requests and questions can, as I say, send an agent, sobbing bitterly, out of his chair to see which is harder—his head or the wall. I'd like to discuss and attempt to clarify a few of the more recurrent insanity inspirers, and in that way, perhaps, straighten out some points in the minds of those of you who are contemplating getting agents but don't quite understand their operating methods.

• The enclosed novel has been rejected by a total of forty-seven publishing companies. I know, however, that you agents have influence with editors and publishers, so please sell it for me as soon as possible.

There isn't an agent in the business who has ever sold a bad script because of personal friendship or influence with an editor or publisher. Most agents have no objection to seeing heavily rejected scripts because they feel they may do a better job of market selection than the author has done, and not because they hope that influence will turn the trick even if the script is a poor one. If that was your reason for thinking of signing up with an agent, you'd better forget about it.

The only reason an agent is able to sell a script is that the story is a good and salable script. No agent is better than the clients he represents—and no agent has ever been able to sell a poor script because he happens to be an agent.

With similar scripts of equal value, sometimes editorial friendship will tip the scales. But if an editor begins to buy poor stuff from an agent friend, the overpowering odor of the material will soon come to the publisher's attention—and the editor will go out on his ear. What, then, would be the point in the carefully cultivated friendship some writers think agents spend their time building? And if the agent's friendship is with the publisher himself, even the publisher can't buy sickening stuff—or the reading public will not buy the books he publishes and will instead give their dollars to publishers who don't have an unscrupulous agent friend.

An agent, generally speaking, has three values as far as the writer is concerned: (1) If he's honest and on the level, he can furnish you with frank evaluations of your stuff, tell you truthfully and expertly about your weak points and strong points—something your family and friends will not or cannot do. (2) He spends every working day in the publishing area—visiting editors, talking to editors on the phone, lunching with editors, sometimes lugging his wife over for games of bridge with editors and their wives. Because of this, he knows the day-by-day things that go on in the field—which houses are buying heavily and which are temporarily stocked, and particular tastes and taboos and eccentricities of editors and publishers—and he can bring you better deals on your material, perhaps contracts with better houses than the ones for which you planned your scripts, and up-to-the-minute trend tips. (3) Equally important, he is a third person. If you write an editor and tell him how superb your script really is, or how much you deserve a big advance, you sound conceited and may antagonize him—even if your script *is* good, or if you *do* deserve a big advance. But an agent may do this because he's not talking about his own work: if he's enthusiastic about a script or asks for more money, it's all right.

> • I don't want an agent who acts as a messenger service. Please inform me by Express Mail whether or not you submit in person everything you handle.

Of course I don't—and it's about time that fond illusion is dispelled. No agent submits in person all the material he handles.

If his morning mail turns up a novel that he thinks is the best he's ever read and which he feels will become an ageless classic, there's no question in the world but that he'll telephone an editor and talk ecstatically about it, or make an appointment with an editor and go over and plug the script to the skies. If a really good nonfiction book comes in, he'll surely telephone a few editors to determine their attitude toward the subject before sending it along. Or if a script of the length and type an editor has requested comes along, or a script by a writer in whom the agent has interested an editor, of course the agent will phone and say, "Joe, I'm sending over Sam McFoop's novel," or "Bill, I've got an appointment near your office. I'll stop by and give you a really excellent science fiction novel that's just come in."

But as far as the usual case is concerned—well, large agencies like mine have a messenger staff, and a few employ the same government men in gray you use when you send your material directly to publishers. If a script rates special attention or heralding of some kind, you may be sure it will get it, through an attached note, a phone call, or a personal visit—but when the script is a typically good script, just right for a house and exactly like others in that respect, there's nothing to be accomplished by personal delivery.

The value of an agent's "messenger service," of course, is that it's his business to know exactly where the script must go. The unagented writer may send a mystery to a house whose inventory is loaded with mysteries, or a nonfiction book to a house that has just contracted for or published a similar book, but the good agent, who—himself and through his staff—keeps up to the second on market information, will almost never do this. He'll know that another house is in need of mysteries, and he'll know another house likely to snap up a nonfiction book on your subject, and you'll have a sale instead of a perhaps unexplained rejection.

• Tell me, do you think it's true that agents who charge fees are off the level? My cousin works in a bar, and a writer who used to come in there and cadge drinks told him that a good agent doesn't charge fees.

No, kiddo, I don't think it's true. You see, *we* charge fees ourselves for reading, analyzing, and making detailed reports on scripts by unestablished writers.

During the earlier days of my agency, we charged no fees for one simple reason: we accepted only established writers with established reputations. There was no reason under the sun to charge fees to examine and report on incoming stuff: our clients had sold enough to justify the conclusion that their output would almost always be salable, and we knew we'd derive our profit from the commission on sales. We knew, too, that the commissions would be regular enough to cover all overhead and pay off the butcher and baker as well.

Some agencies work that way today. They handle the top names only and won't handle you until you become a top name yourself, and they don't charge fees because, when you're added to their list, your stuff is so professional and your sales chances always so good that it isn't necessary. They've got an important and urgent place in the field—they take business worries off the hands of busy professionals.

I decided to add promising new writers to our agency list because, in the course of an expansion program some years ago, I hired several additional staff members who were fresh and bright and full of good ideas. An agency built of household-name clients is a fine thing, they pointed out, but to add only writers who have already arrived is a halfway measure. There are many fine writers who never arrive because of poor market sense or because nobody ever gets around to straightening out the technical flaws in their stuff—and if newer writers could be sifted through and the promising people *groomed* for major success, it would easily be worthwhile. This was in line with my own thinking, and I agreed, provided overhead would be covered while the grooming is going on.

That phrase—"provided overhead be covered"—is the answer to fees, and the reason agents charge them. Newer writers may believe they know technique backward and forward, but in many cases it turns out that they've misunderstood or misinterpreted the rules and their stuff is full of holes. These errors must be corrected: the agent and his staff must write long letters of advice and analysis, pushing the newcomer's stuff into proper channels, until he straightens out and begins to sell. And even these beginning sales mean nothing, for until the sales become steady and regular, the time spent in the selling eats up the profit.

During this period, the agent must be paid for the time spent away from his arrived clients—his staff must be paid, his electricity and stationery and telephone bills must be covered. Most agents, you will find, charge fees that obviously cover only overhead—and the proof of the pudding is in the fact that all agents drop fees after they make several deals for a client.

Our decision to handle new writers as well as established people, incidentally, was one of the happiest moves we've ever made, since so very many of the top writers on our list today first came to us in that way: with no sales at all to their credit. And that, of course, is the reason we now have an absolute policy of pushing a new writer's script as hard as scripts by our biggest names: we know through pleasant experience that the new writer, whose scripts today bring in small commissions, may well be the man or woman writing the hot, big-money properties tomorrow.

Unfortunately, agency fees aren't small, overhead costs being what they are these days (and I write this line with the sincerity and fervor of a man who has done what I've just done, which is sign a new lease that makes our monthly rental exactly four times as much as it was under our previous lease; and it wasn't low under the previous lease, either). The average agency fee for short stories or articles runs about $150 minimum fee per script of under ten thousand words, and flat rates for books are generally about $250 for books of average length (under 100,000 words), $300 for books from 100,000 to below 200,000 words, $400 for gigantic books from 200,000 to 300,000 words, and $600 for super-super-giants above 300,000 words. This usually includes all service—reading, detailed analysis and report, assistance and advice for necessary revisions, marketing, etc. The only additional charge is the commission upon sale of the manuscript, which is the same as that charged on scripts by established writers: ten percent on deals made with United States markets, and twenty percent on deals made with

British, French, and other foreign markets. (This matter of total representation in all areas, both domestic and foreign, incidentally, is an extremely important one, because sales possibilities are so complex and widespread today that only a specialist such as a really experienced agent can handle the job efficiently. An agent's job is only beginning when he makes a deal on your book with an American publisher. Aside from overseeing and assisting wherever possible in the various domestic areas—serialization in a magazine before book publication, advertising and promotion after book publication, the eventual paperback reprint, book club deals, motion picture and television deals, and the like—he also goes to work to arrange for separate and additional editions to be published by foreign firms around the world. And on some books, separate deals can be made in thirty different countries.) One warning: about a dozen agencies have recently raised their commission to fifteen percent on domestic deals. My own agency and a lot of others, however, remain at ten percent; we do fine at ten percent by getting bigger and better deals for our clients.

> • I understand that you handle on straight commission basis writers who have been selling regularly. I've sold $620 worth of news reporting to *Feed Grinder,* and now I want to write humorous novels. I presume you'll handle me on straight commission basis and without fee charges. What do you say?

Usually I say "No," for this fellow doesn't really understand the purpose of fees, and probably suspects agents invented them just to annoy him personally.

We charge a fee in the first place because we want our basic expenses to be covered while we're working with a writer who hasn't proved himself through steady sales—and we skip fees with a writer who has been getting published because we feel that he's proved himself sufficiently professional to take the chance of working with him without coverage of overhead through fees because we believe we'll cover our costs and make a profit through sales of new scripts. But the point is that, if we're not going to charge him coverage-of-overhead fees, he must have a sales record that will justify it.

The fact that a writer has achieved considerable success in trade news reporting doesn't give any clue at all to his abilities as a writer of light fiction. He may be a dud or he may be a master; but, if he should turn out to be a dud, we can't afford to analyze his stuff and work him into fiction markets without charge simply because he's a great success in a totally different field.

If a successful genre writer wants to try to switch to mainstream novels, for example, I'm always happy to take him on, on commission—because one kind of fiction is in its elements much like all other fiction, and the two are close enough. If a popular novelist wants us to handle her unexpected book of sentimental verse, that's all right—and we're happy to do it, for the commissions on her novels cover the additional expense of selling a book of verse at one thousand dollars advance, or possibly even five hundred dollars, and the author's soul is at peace.

But if you've had some success in one field and want to go into an entirely different one, don't expect an agent to work his head off breaking you into the new field without payment of fees.

• Hiss, hiss. You returned my novel, *He Done Killed Her Dead,* with a letter explaining why it's unsalable. You'll be amazed to hear that *Independent Corn-Pone Grower* has just bought the first chapter and scheduled it for their Fall–Winter issue.

My reaction to this sort of thing is generally, Great going, pal, and many more—but the *Independent Corn-Pone Grower* pays only twenty bucks for material.

Although some writers do not realize it, it must be understood by you that a literary agency is not entirely a benevolent association, but is engaged in making money so that the owner and his staff keep off skid row. And the commission on a twenty-dollar sale, I can tell you without pausing to count on my fingers, is only two dollars—not even enough these days to buy permission to step into a restaurant and sniff deeply.

Occasionally an agent will make a sale to a very minor market because the script won't sell to any of the better ones, and the writer is either a newcomer who can use the emotional stimulus of a sale, or an old-timer who can use the money in any shape, form, or amount. But there's a limit to these things: obviously, when an agent has exhausted all the best markets and all the fair ones, he simply can't afford to continue with the tiny ones—and once in a while a script sells to these tiny ones, the markets to which the agent can't afford to submit. Don't misunderstand: this doesn't mean that agents give up quickly. Quite the contrary, in fact. There *are,* sadly, a very few nitwit agents around who set limits on their submissions, and give up and return a script to an author if, for example, it doesn't sell after five tries, but most agencies, including my own, will try and try and *try* until they succeed. We hope for and are usually successful in selling scripts first time out or at least second time out, but there have been a few instances in which we've gone to seventy publishers, and even more, in order to make a sale.

Have the same consideration for the agent he tries to have for you. Don't ask him to handle your output if you plan to specialize in fillers, or religious-market material, which sell for a few dollars apiece. And don't expect him to continue trying your short story right down to the experimental journals, which pay their writers with subscriptions. An agent who tries to pay his rent with ten percent of subscriptions will quickly find himself outside his office building.

Another answer to the fact that writers sometimes sell work returned by agents is that the Lord never quite got around to making any of us perfect. A very good agent I know received a script from a client who was a comparatively new writer, and didn't like it too much, but he took it to a publishing house anyhow because the editors there were especially receptive to newcomers. When the house returned it with a cold comment, he decided his original opinion had been backed up, and returned the script to its author. The author sent it off to another top house, which promptly contracted for it.

When you consider, however, that this was the agent's second major error in judgment in nearly fourteen years, you've got to admit that the record isn't a bad one.

* Please send me eleven bank references, your certificate of citizenship, and a sworn statement testifying that you've been vaccinated against inflamed gums. I was recently gypped by another New York agent, and I'm afraid that you may be a dangerous criminal, too.

The answer to that one is that there have been thieves and incompetents in every industry and profession from bootblacking to banking to bazooka-making to the presidency of the United States—and it seems somewhat overimaginative to express concern about an unrelated person or company in a field because another individual in the field is a bad 'un. Jack the Ripper was possibly an editor during the daytime, as a disgruntled writer once assured me, but there are still some awfully nice men and women among editors.

Generally speaking, an agent who has many established professionals among his clients is bound to be honest and reliable—because writers pass the word around quickly when an agent is shady, and the shady agent's list quickly dissolves or never gets built up. There's one way to find out about an agent's clients, incidentally: write and ask him. If he's got a good client list, he'll be proud of his clients and answer you promptly and fully; if he's evasive, beware.

Occasionally, of course, an agent who has worked honorably for writers for years will suddenly start to pull all kinds of stunts, as was the case with one some years ago. This is the sort of thing that no one can predict—and is perhaps caused by temporary or permanent insanity, glandular trouble, or an overdose of Serutan. It's in the class with bank tellers who are honest for twenty years and suddenly rush off with a satchelful of money, and is a chance you must take—like the chance you take when you turn in a suit or a dress to the dry cleaner's. He may be gone, clothing and all, the next morning; but if he's been in business for a while and has a reputation for honesty, the chances are that he won't.

> • I sent you a script on Monday, and here it is Thursday and I haven't heard from you. What's the matter—you lose my script or something?

No, we haven't, friend. We're still working on it, so keep cool.

Most agencies begin work on material almost immediately after its arrival. After the script has been carded and otherwise registered, it's turned over to the agency head or his staff for reading, and if immediately salable is taken to market.

Sometimes, however, it isn't. It displays certain important flaws, yet at the same time it displays a lot of good writing and some evident ability. That makes it a problem: it isn't quite right to take to market, it can't be returned for a rewrite because the fault is in the basic framework itself and that would amount to writing an entirely new script, and yet it isn't bad enough to be returned with suggestion to destroy. There's a staff meeting called; sometimes, when the script is really a puzzler, two or three meetings. All this takes time, for though the script may be enough of a hair-grayer to interest everybody, discussions and meetings on it must be sandwiched between work on other pressing matters. The average agency report is sent within two weeks, and many times (as is the case with established professionals, whose scripts can usually go out to market immediately) even by return mail, but you must realize that work is being performed for your own good even if a month passes without report.

And if a script is okayed and sent to market, the agent can't send the writer a play-by-play description of what's happening to it, though he will, of course, inform the writer initially that it has gone out. The agent reports to the author whenever he has news—a deal, a requested rewrite from an editor, an important editorial comment, or something of that sort. He just can't, however, inform the author each time a script has not made the grade at a market and gone to another, or he'd have no time to do anything else. It would also not be a good idea for an agent to inform an author of every rejection, or every few rejections, because some authors, not being in the thick of the battle, would become suicidal at the avalanche of bad news, or at least certain that their material is lousy. An agent, however, knows better because he sometimes sees very good scripts take a while to sell. And he's also more detached because the scripts aren't his own creations, so he can continue to do his job with calmness until he succeeds.

Generally, for the reason of the rush-and-unrush system, plus the fact that agents who consistently take good material to editors will naturally get prompter attention, literary agents get fast reports on material they send to market. Sometimes, however, editors get bogged down with other work and take longer in their reporting; in those cases, the agent's only choice is to prod them gently as much as possible but mostly grin and bear it. And then, of course, the agent's own report to you of eventual acceptance will be slower in coming.

Just remember that the key to happiness lies in that adage laid down long, long ago: if you want to stay sane, forget about a script the moment it leaves your home, and concentrate on new material.

If you decide to submit directly to publishing houses instead of working through an agent, there are two things you must do to familiarize yourself with market needs and otherwise keep in touch with your business. First, read the published works in the field for which you're aiming, and read them carefully. And second, get yourself a subscription to the bible of the publishing industry, *Publishers Weekly,* and buy yourself a copy of a good marketing guide such as *Literary Market Place,* which is published by the same company. (The preceding plug is because they're good. I'm not connected with them in any way and I don't own even a tiny fragment of the company, though I wish I did. The parent company is an obscure little organization named Xerox.)

Magazines like *Publishers Weekly* are to writers what medical journals and magazines like *Medical Economics* are to doctors: they serve as clearinghouses for information on publishing firms, the kinds of books that are succeeding with the general public and the kinds that aren't, new methods that publishers are using to advertise and promote and sell books, and all other information of value to the worker in the field. In addition, these publications report important events in the publishing world such as prize contests and the birth of new markets and from time to time publish full lists of all publishers and their needs in new or relatively new fields like computer books or audio publishing (the latter being tapes in which actors or authors read the important sections of novels or nonfiction books and summarize the in-between parts that they don't read. You buy these tapes and listen, for example, in your car while driving.).

When you get your specific choice of markets down pat, there are several things to keep in mind about the marketing itself.

Try to keep yourself, first of all, from becoming discouraged and giving up on a script because it piles up a few rejections. Sometimes a script hits the right market at the right moment and sells at first submission, or within two or three submissions, as agents' submissions often do; other scripts just as good may take a lot of offering around before they're accepted. Almost everyone who has been in the writing business for some time can think of dozens of cases of manuscripts that had been rejected at market after market and then were finally accepted. (*The Godfather* is just one example that comes to mind; it went begging from house to house before it was finally published and became a monumental best-seller.) I've also mentioned the rare instances in which we've had to submit a script endlessly in order to sell it, and we've just added one more case to the file.

A number of months ago, my agency took on a novel that was an odd sort of script and which we knew would be hard to sell, but which we liked very much, and we offered it to forty markets without acceptance or even encouragement. The forty-first market bought it gladly, paid a top price for it, and subsequently we showed an outstanding motion picture producer the book in galleys and he's bought the movie rights. Negotiations have also been concluded for the author to do the screenplay for the film, thus adding a large screen-writing fee to the healthy amounts the author has already received from the book advance and purchase of film rights.

The point is that if you have real faith in a script, keep it going to market after market until every logical possibility has been exhausted.

I might add, also, that although it is considered unethical to submit a story to more than one magazine at a time, because of the irritations and mix-ups that might occur if you sent out several copies of the same story and several different editors bought the story simultaneously, it's becoming increasingly acceptable, for several reasons, to submit copies of book manuscripts to more than one house at a time. The first reason has to do with the difference between book and magazine purchasing procedures. The process of contracting for your material is much more involved and time-consuming in the book field than with magazines, and there really is no danger that several houses could complete purchase simultaneously or even feel morally that they'd "acquired" your book. Second, as publishing houses continue to merge, sometimes growing smaller in number and staff but larger in the totals of books they publish each season, editors are having to face the fact that, with the increased number of submissions to each house, the delays in reading and reporting on submitted scripts are increasing, and the author will occasionally feel that he has to protect his interests by submitting to a few houses instead of just one. Third, and actually the most important, some agencies (I'll admit that we were the first) have cleared the way for this practice by pioneering multiple submissions on our most important and hottest properties, pitting publishers against each other in competitive bidding and thereby "testing the market" and determining the best deal possible (the largest advance available, for example, and other considerations such as the likelihood of the most knowledgeable advertising and promotion for the particular kind of book involved) on each book offered in that way.

No matter where and how you market your script, remember that it isn't wise to inform an editor that a script has previously been seen and rejected by others. However fairminded he may be, and however much he may feel that he wants what he wants and doesn't care whether or not others wanted it, he may still form an unconscious prejudice against it.

Make sure, too, that you keep careful records of the markets to which you have submitted each script: you don't want to forget and return a script to an editor who's already seen and rejected it. The only time it is really safe to resubmit a script to a house that has already seen it is when you read in *Publishers Weekly* that there has been a reorganization there and the staff has substantially changed.

28

JUST SIGN HERE, PLEASE
Contracts, Rights, and Other Legal Matters

Since all of the previous chapters in this book have been designed to help you land a publishing contract for your script, it's only fair that I tell you what to expect in the contract itself. Book contracts are formidable-looking documents that run anywhere from a couple of pages to sixty or seventy, and the language in them can seem like Sanskrit to a beginner. But the fact is that, like almost everything else, a book contract is really not so difficult to understand once you get past appearances into the substance of the thing.

Although publishers' contracts vary in details, and in the order in which they present the terms, you'll find that the major features are pretty much the same from house to house. Let's take a guided tour of a typical book publishing agreement and see what there is to see in its various provisions.

All contracts start out routinely by naming the parties to the agreement—the publisher and you—your addresses, the date of the agreement, and the tentative title of the script that the publisher is buying. In instances where a contract is given for a book still in progress and not yet completed, a few houses also include a brief description of the book after the title, something like this: *"The Evangelist,* a novel about a college professor who leads his students into revolutionary activities." That's just to make absolutely certain that the book for which they're contracting doesn't change without warning into a novel about a traveling country preacher.

Following this opening section, usually, is one of the most crucial parts of the contract, the grant of rights to the publisher. The primary right granted to the publisher is, of course, the exclusive right to publish the material in book form in the United States, although this grant usually broadens the definition of the territory beyond the United States, to include Canada, United States Possessions, and the Philippines. Great Britain and the Commonwealth constitute a very important and separate book-buying market, and I urge you to struggle hard here to retain these rights for yourself, since you can then make a second, substantial deal for publication of your book there. Sometimes the publisher will state the rights granted to him simply as "World English Rights" or "World English Language Rights"; this means including the British Empire, so watch out for this phrase. You'll have to make your own decision on whether or not you finally end up granting the British Empire, since a few houses, such as some of the small paperback firms, just won't contract unless they get World English Language Rights. But it's important, at the very least, to be aware of what you're granting.

After establishing the publisher's basic territory, the contract goes on to grant the publisher the right to license other uses of your material; these other rights are usually called "subsidiary rights," and licensing simply means that the publisher allows other firms to use these rights for a share of the take. Subsidiary rights include reprint rights, mostly meaning the eventual paperback editions of your book, book club rights, foreign translation rights, motion picture rights, radio and television rights, various uses of the work in magazines and other periodicals (serial rights), and so on.

Income from paperback reprint editions and book club editions are generally shared fifty-fifty between author and publisher, though agents have recently begun to get better than fifty percent of paperback money for their most eminent clients, and have also begun to cast an interested and hungry eye at the book club money. (I'll also boast a little here and tell you that my agency was the first to get a hardcover publisher to accept less than a fifty percent share of paperback revenue.

Until then, it was the absolute rule for paperback income to be shared equally between the author and his or her hardcover publisher, and the word from every hardcover publisher was "no exceptions—you hear me?" This was a rule that rankled because of one very well-known client whose sales were modest in hardcover editions but huge in their eventual paperback reprints, and I just couldn't convince him to forget about hardcover and have his books done as paperback originals, so that he could keep all the revenue instead of only half, because he wanted those hardcover editions on his shelves to show his kids. I finally went to the author's hardcover publisher and did some tough talking, saying that I understood his company's right to have a large share of the paperback revenue because they launched each book and advertised and promoted it and made it visible—but that *didn't* give the company the right to be the author's equal partner. Then I went on and told the publisher that, if he didn't agree, we'd move the author to another house that would accept a smaller paperback share. It was a bloody battle, but we won the war, and today an important or upcoming author or an agent can, at all but a couple of publishing houses, negotiate a 60/40 deal in the author's favor, and sometimes a 70/30 deal, and occasionally even an 80/20 deal.)

The shares on motion picture money, foreign translation money, and the like vary from house to house; some houses ask no share at all, some ask only five or ten percent, and some try for the same half share as on paperback and book club. Don't try to retain paperback or book club rights for yourself; this has become so important a part of the picture that some hardcover houses would go out of business without their share of this money, and there've only been a couple of instances in publishing where authors with truly blockbuster hardcover sales were able to sell hardcover rights only. But if you've got a good agent, or you're a pretty good negotiator personally, you can nearly always retain one hundred percent of the other subsidiary rights, like motion picture and foreign rights, for yourself. My agency and others have a very simple policy in this area: we don't give publishers any share of these rights, period.

If you made your deal on the basis of a partial manuscript, a portion-and-outline, the contract will name a delivery date for the full script and will stipulate that the script must be satisfactory to the publisher in form and content. Some newer writers fret over the idea of being pinned down to a specific date and of giving the publisher the right to reject the final script and require return of all money, but there is really no reason to worry. Although you should take the publisher's deadline very seriously—and your reputation in the business can only be enhanced by a consistent record of prompt deliveries—the publisher will invariably stretch the deadline if unforeseen circumstances cause a delay, and if your editor is convinced that you're working steadily on the script. About the only time the delivery clause is ever invoked to cancel the contract is when it becomes apparent that you're never going to finish that script, or that you will, but only after your editor writes you another eighty-two reminder letters.

The part of the delivery clause specifying that the script must be satisfactory to the publisher is also very seldom a problem, since the publisher's staff has generally seen a substantial portion of the script plus a detailed outline describing the material to come, and know what they're getting. It's not unusual to see a request for a few revisions, but the flat rejection of a script under contract is extremely rare. It happens only when the author has fallen down on the job to a serious degree and turned in a clearly half-hearted effort; in all other cases, your editor will help you along, if necessary, and will not invoke the delivery clause.

Another standard part of the book contract is the "date, style, and price" provision, in which your publisher promises to bring the book out within a specified period—usually a year to eighteen months—after receipt of the full script. This is a sort of guarantee that your book won't languish endlessly in inventory before receiving a fair trial in the marketplace. This section also reserves for your publisher the right to determine the book's selling price and style of publication. Newer authors sometimes have strong ideas about how their book should be presented, and worry about letting a bunch of strangers determine the physical appearance of the book, but these fears are almost always groundless. The people who do the cover art, select typeface and paper, and write the jacket copy are people who do that and only that for a living. They're professionals, and while they may not lavish quite the attention on your cover that Michelangelo gave to the ceiling of the Sistine Chapel, they generally do an excellent and intelligent job.

The bread-and-butter section of the contract, of course, is the one that covers money, and that's the royalty section. The first part of this section spells out the amount of your advance against royalties, and the manner in which it's to be paid. As mentioned earlier, a typical advance for a first novel might range between twenty-five hundred and ten thousand dollars, but the advance for a big property by an established author can easily involve hundreds of thousands or even millions of dollars; you've undoubtedly read of my agency's deal for Dr. Carl Sagan's first novel, *Contact,* for an advance of $2,000,000, or of the recent deal for James Clavell involving $5,000,000. No matter what the size of the advance, it's nonreturnable, unless you violate one of the contract's basic warranties, which we'll discuss later, or fail to deliver a satisfactory script.

The advance can be paid in any number of ways: half on signing of the contract and half on delivery of the script, if the script isn't yet completed; all on signing, if the script is in hand; a third on signing, a third on delivery, and a third on publication, as in some paperback deals; and so on. Often, if there's a lot of money involved and the author would prefer not to receive it all at once, some of the money will be paid on signing and the rest paid in installments on specific dates, sometimes stretching for several years into the future.

Despite the nonreturnable feature, the advance *is* an advance, a loan against the book's projected income, and you won't receive any royalties until the amount of the advance has accrued in your account, or, in the common phrase, until after the advance has been "earned out."

Your contract will next spell out the royalty rate for your book, which means the percentage of the retail price of the book credited to you. Like the advance, the royalty rate can vary considerably from book to book, but a ballpark figure for hardcover is from ten percent to fifteen percent, and higher in rare cases, and from four percent to fifteen percent in typical paperback deals, and higher in a very few special cases. A graduated scale is generally used. On hardcover deals for newer authors, for example, the standard royalty is ten percent on the first five thousand copies sold, twelve and one-half percent on the next five thousand copies, and fifteen percent thereafter; major authors generally get fifteen percent on every copy sold. In paperback, a typical graduated scale would specify a six percent rate for the first 150,000 copies sold, and eight percent thereafter. The contract goes on to set special royalty rates for special kinds of sales, like mail order, educational, and export sales. The rates on these sales are usually lower, but there's no need to worry that the publisher will encourage them at your expense, since the publisher generally sells these copies in bulk at discounts and earns less from them, too.

The publisher promises, elsewhere in the contract, to prepare statements of sales and royalties for specified periods, such as those ending on April 1 and October 1 of each year, and to give you these statements, and any moneys due, within, say, four months after each period ends. This means that if your publisher has compiled statistics on sales of your book for the period ending April 1, you'll receive a statement and any moneys that are due no later than August 1. The four-month period is needed to gather the statistics and to make sure that your earnings from sales in Minneapolis haven't been wiped out by returns from bookstores in Boston, since books are always sold to wholesalers and to stores on a fully returnable basis. (If there appears to be a good chance that returns of unsold books might be forthcoming, the publisher has the right, specified in the contract, to hold some of your royalties as a "reserve against returns." In other words, if you've earned out your advance and have earned another ten thousand dollars in royalties in the latest period, and the publisher feels that as much as two thousand dollars' worth of unsold copies might be coming back to him soon, he has the right to hold two thousand dollars of your royalties against returns, and pay you eight thousand dollars. If the returns turn out to be a false alarm and don't materialize, you'll get the reserved money after the end of the next royalty period.) Also included in your royalty statement and payment as royalty money will be your share of the income from the publisher's sale of the subsidiary rights you granted.

Somewhere in every contract, often near the beginning, is the author's warranty. It's a vital clause in which you warrant that you're really the original author of the material you're selling, and that you're authorized, therefore, to grant the publisher the rights given in the contract. It means that if your material turns out to be taken or plagiarized from someone else (or, as contracts put it politely, if your material is "in violation of any copyright"), the contract is null and void, and you'll have to return all money paid to you and also reimburse the publisher for any printing and production costs incurred. The warranty also includes your guarantee that the material isn't libelous and doesn't invade anybody's privacy.

There is in addition an indemnity clause in which you agree to hold the publisher harmless from any damage claims sustained as a result of any violation of your warranty. The indemnity clause also specifies the sharing of legal expenses in the event that a defense of the book is needed, but, as a practical matter, most publishers realize that they're richer than most authors and pick up all the costs in cases where there's a lawsuit and where the accusations prove groundless. In instances, obviously, where you're sued and you turn out to be guilty, your publisher won't be as generous.

In a separate clause, usually called the "conflicting publication" clause, you agree that you won't allow someone else to publish your book or material from it in book form without your publisher's consent. This understanding is implied by the grant of rights and exclusive territory to the publisher, but this clause makes it explicit. It is designed to protect the publisher in situations like the following one: let's say you've written a book on the collecting of Japanese netsuke, and a fellow-collector has written a book on the same subject, and wants to quote copiously from your book in his. You may be willing to grant him permission to do this even though the two books will be coming out at the same time, but the publisher may feel that doing so will injure the sales of your book and thereby his profits, so this clause gives him the right to prohibit your grant.

Elsewhere in the contract, the publisher agrees to take out copyright in your name, or if copyright must be taken out in the publisher's name—if, for example, you write under a pen name and want to keep your name secret—the publisher agrees to assign copyright to you upon request. The publisher also agrees to send you free copies of the book—usually between six and twelve copies—and to allow you to buy further copies at a substantial discount, usually forty percent off the cover price.

If you quote copyrighted material in your book, most contracts say that you're responsible for securing from the copyright owner and paying for permission to use that material. Another clause states that you'll be sent galley sheets for proofreading, and that if you require changes beyond the mere correction of printers' errors—if, for example, you decide to revise the book heavily after it's in galleys—the publisher will pick up ten percent of the cost of resetting type and you'll have to pay the rest.

One of the more important provisions in any book contract is the option clause, in which you're asked to agree to give the publisher first chance to consider your next script. The contract usually sets a period of about six weeks from the day of your submission of the script, in which time the publisher will decide whether or not to make an offer for it, and then another few weeks for the purpose of coming to an agreement on terms. If you can't agree on terms, you're free to sell the script elsewhere, as long as you don't accept terms that are inferior to those offered by your first publisher.

Sometimes, under special circumstances, the option clause has to be struck or modified. If, for example, you're established as a mainstream novelist but you've taken up a sideline of writing occasional mystery novels for another house, your mystery book contract's option clause may have to be modified to apply only to your next genre novel, so that it doesn't interfere with your relationship with the house that does your general novels. Or, if you're an increasingly popular author and you and your agent have good reason to feel that you may want to try to move to another house next time, on much better terms, you may want to try to get the option clause eliminated.

All contracts contain a kind of "self-destruct" clause, providing for a "reversion of rights" to you in the event that the publisher allows the book to go out of print. In that event, you or your agent are generally required to make a written request for a return of rights, and the publisher must then either bring out or license another edition of the book or return the rights to you. If your contract is with a hardcover house, incidentally, and there is a paperback edition—or any other edition—in print in your publisher's territory, then the book is considered not yet out of print. But if it does go out of print, and the publisher decides not to bring it back into print after receiving your request, the contract expires, and the rights to the book revert to you, and you're free to sell it again.

The final section of the contract is usually the "agency clause," which is included if you have an agent. The clause acknowledges the fact that the money due under the contract will be paid to your agent for transmittal to you, that he's authorized to act on your behalf in all matters arising out of the agreement, and that he'll retain a standard commission on all sums paid.

Here's the most valuable piece of advice anyone will ever give you on the matter of contracts that seem too complex to understand: don't try to figure them out all by yourself. If you have an agent, he'll explain the details of your contracts to you, and see that you get a good one; but if you don't have an agent, go to a good lawyer. Most publishing contracts today are honest and aboveboard, but the legal mind sees things a bit differently from the lay mind, and you may find yourself in trouble or disappointed if you misunderstand or misinterpret some of the clauses.

The best attorney for advice on involved contracts—and on all other publishing problems for that matter—is one who specializes in publishing affairs. If you live in or around New York City, the local office of the American Bar Association will recommend several. If you don't, see a general practitioner—but in that case, go for interpretation rather than advice. There are too many angles and special aspects in the writing business that a man outside it may not know or consider. Just get the attorney to explain each clause in simple, nonlegal language and, by measuring these against the yardstick of your own experience in the writing business, decide for yourself whether or not the contract is fair.

29

ANOTHER HORIZON
Nonfiction

Writers who begin with novels and short stories sometimes discover that they're also interested in doing nonfiction books and articles, and occasionally you'll find that a well-known writer of fiction has switched over entirely to the nonfiction field. The market for nonfiction and the earnings possible in it are comparable to the situation in fiction writing. You may want to enter this field yourself, so let's have a look at it.

There are three principal types of nonfiction that sell today: the opinion book, the educational-helpful book, and the amusement-entertainment book. We'll examine each kind in turn.

The opinion book is exactly what it sounds like: one man's personal ideas and views on a subject. Into this class would go such books as *What We Must Do About the Mideast, Let's Give Up on Space Travel,* and others along the same lines.

The important thing to remember about the opinion book is that the views and ideas expressed therein must be backed up by a special authority on the subject. Once in a very great while, a publisher will receive an especially perceptive and original-thinking script from a nonauthority, and will buy and publish it—often with a title that points up the writer's lack of special authority (such as *A Housewife Versus the Government* or *A Taxpayer's Challenge to Congress*) plus an ad campaign that states enthusiastically that "everyday people" can do sensible thinking on the popular topics and problems of the day, too. These books are the rare exceptions to the rule: the other nine hundred and ninety-nine known books out of each thousand by everyday people get the quick heave-ho into the rejection stack.

The editor realizes, in a nutshell, that today's facilities for mass dissemination of information have made the average reader pretty perceptive and knowledgeable on popular or controversial topics, so that he doesn't particularly care to hear opinions on the subjects from people like himself who have acquired the information in the same way he has—through newspapers, radio and television, other books, and the like. He wants books from people on the inside, people with special or additional knowledge—in other words, from recognized authorities on the subject.

It's pretty foolish, therefore, and almost always a waste of valuable writing time, to do opinion books under your own byline if you are not a recognized authority on some important or interesting subject. The way the nonauthority professional writer fits into the opinion-book picture is by doing the book for the authority—either under the authority's lone byline or under a dual, as-told-to byline (for example, *Monkeys and Man,* by John C. Anthropologist, as told to Amanda Author).

Your initial impression may be that this leaves you out if you don't know any authorities or live in a small town, but actually that isn't the case. One of our clients, for instance, specializes in opinion books by authorities and earns over $100,000 a year writing them, despite the fact that he lives in a small Midwestern town and did not know a single authority personally when he started out. He arranged with a reporter on a newspaper in the nearest large town to tip him off (for a small sum per tip) when a nationally famous figure arrived for a brief stay—a well-known political figure, or a millionaire tycoon, or a famous figure in sports or motion pictures. When someone who interested him came to town, he sat down and thought of a good controversial topic in line with the authority's profession on which the authority would very likely be interested in expressing himself. And then he phoned the celebrity or his secretary and said that he wanted to work with the authority on a book on the subject, stressing heavily the good public relations that would result from publication of such a book. In almost every case, particularly after he'd had a few books published and could name the books on which he'd collaborated and the celebrities with whom he'd worked, he was told to come along and discuss it—and he often emerged with permission to do the book. On such collaborations, the division of earnings between celebrity and author is nearly always a matter of friendly but firm negotiation. Some celebrities insist on a fifty-fifty split of proceeds, and others will cooperate strictly for prestige and publicity and allow the author to keep most of the income, so of course the object is to get as close to the latter arrangement as possible. Your agent will also handle the negotiation with the celebrity or authority, of course, if you have an agent.

As in everything else in life, the toughest time for the would-be opinion-book writer is the breaking-in period—many well-known people are unwilling to waste time or work with an unestablished author. Some won't even be willing to *discuss* the notion of collaboration with an unknown author. Your best argument against this is a sincere and strong sales talk: to the effect that your meeting with them won't take too long, that at worst they'll only waste a little time and at best gain valuable publicity, and that you're trying to break in and make a living, and how about a break? It will often do the trick.

The educational-helpful book is also exactly what its name says: it is the book that helps while it educates. It's the personal-application book, the book with "you" appeal.

Typical educational-helpful books are the profit-by-my-experience-and-do-this (or-don't-do-that) type (for example, *My Life as a Widow, I Regained My Family's Respect, I Was an Alcoholic,* etc.), which are, in a way, opinion books backed with the authority of personal experience; the everyday-psychology type (such as *Don't Pamper Your Children* or *How to Build a Happy Marriage*), though you'd better make *these* recognized-authority's-opinion books and get a doctor or a psychologist to sign them if you go deeper than common sense and logic and into technical psychology; useful-information books (such as *Make Money as a Photographer of Children* and *How to Build Lamps from Old Bottles*); and books that give new information on a new slant of *personal* importance to the reader and his way of life (for example, *Will a Tax Shelter Help You?* or *We Can Stop Racial Prejudice*).

Don't, incidentally, confuse the educational-helpful book with the straight education book, which few publishers bring out these days. At one time, many houses published straight educational books (for example, *How Our Flag Was Born* or *How Silkworms Create Silk*); today (outside of juveniles, where education is a primary purpose) most editors feel that that sort of thing belongs more properly in an encyclopedia, because it has neither sufficient entertainment value nor sufficient personal-application value to sell books. Just keep in mind both halves of the educational-helpful classification, and you won't go wrong.

The greatest pitfall in the educational-helpful book is triteness. Try to choose subjects on which you can present advice or information that have not been given before to the average reader, or at least not too often before. And be sure to choose subjects that will interest the bulk of the audience, rather than just a few members. Most people, for example, are interested in books on money-making and on health subjects, because these are things that may affect them personally, or may affect people who are close to them. It's doubtful, however, that you can sell a book for general audiences on advances in the study of Huntington's chorea, one of the rarest diseases in the world.

The remaining category, amusement-entertainment, covers the factual book whose sole purpose is to divert the reader by telling him about someone or something interesting and unusual. It includes profiles and biographies of colorful and famous people (movie stars, politics, business magnates, and so on); books about interesting organizations (such as a sports team or an international police force); books about people who do unusual things (such as a man who sails around the world alone, or a man who has made a huge fortune from currency devaluations); books about unusual events (such as an unprecedented and ingenious bank robbery, or the time a dictator set out to relax the country's harsh laws); books about unusual places (such as a virtually unexplored area of New Guinea or a nation that forbids development of its natural resources); and so on.

The important aspect of the amusement-entertainment book, and the factor that usually determines its salability or lack of salability, is whether or not its subject is sufficiently unusual and interesting to grip the reader—or, more properly, the varied readers who make up the cross section of book buyers.

Let's say, for example, that you write a book about a woman in your home state who started out with some ideas about millinery but almost no money, and in five years built a millinery business that brings her a personal income of about twenty thousand dollars a year. The story of the woman and her success is interesting, but probably not interesting enough to make the book salable because a great many other people have built similar successes in about the same amount of time and to the same degree. On the other hand, a man who built a multi-million-dollar corporation in a short time and with very little money would make an excellent subject, because his story is sufficiently unusual to grip *any* reader's attention.

The same thing would apply, as another example, to a travel book. If you write a script about your recent trip to Mexico, where you do all the points of interest as recommended by the travel agency, your book will not sell because there's nothing particularly interesting or unusual about it. If, however, you ran into an unusual experience there—you came upon a strange tribe of people in one of the isolated sections, people who can leap twenty-five feet into the air—and you can document this fact to the publisher's editor's satisfaction you've got yourself an amusement-entertainment book that may click. There's a simple yardstick here, by the way. Keep in mind the fact that there's a kind of ground swell against book buying at stores these days, because printing costs are such that even the thinnest books imaginable must be priced at $9.95, and not-too-big books are priced at eighteen or twenty dollars. The result is that many, perhaps most, people no longer buy books casually; they've really got to *want* them. So ask yourself if your projected book is one people will really want— if *you* would pay sixteen or eighteen or twenty dollars for it if you weren't the author. If the answer, genuinely and sincerely, is yes, you're probably on safe ground.

The fact that something is interesting to you and your friends, or to the people in your home area, will not necessarily mean that something is a suitable subject for a salable book. It must be measured against the yardstick of the entire country, and all the different kinds of people in it. If the subject would really be interesting and unusual to everybody, and hasn't already been heavily covered, it should be okay.

From the description of the various types of nonfiction-book subjects in the preceding pages, you've probably realized that, as in fiction, you get book ideas from the things you read, and the things around you, and all the other factors of your own experience.

When you get an idea, you'll know pretty well, from your own reading of current books and the book review column or section of your local newspapers, whether or not the subject has been covered recently, or too often in the past. Make a further check, however; go to your local public library and look up the subject in the card catalog. It won't list every book published, of course, but it will give you a pretty good picture of whether you've hit on something fresh or something that has already been done to death.

30

YOU'RE ON YOUR OWN

In some future superatomic age, perhaps, manuscripts will be written by authorship machines, and a writer will be a sort of engineer who brings forth different types of books on call by pressing different combinations of six or seven buttons. When that's the case, there'll probably also be precision instruments to measure the quality and correctness of the problem, complications, language, transitions, and all the other ingredients that make up a work of fiction.

Today, however, a script is strictly a handmade affair, and the manner in which a script is judged is just as informal and unprecise. Few editors, if any, actually sit down and judge a book by each of its separate components; few, if any, actually say to themselves, in as many words, "Is the problem strong enough? Are the complications worrisome enough? Are the descriptions vivid enough? Are the transitions smooth enough?" It's the total effect, the total reaction, given by a book that usually determines its acceptance or rejection.

You will not, as I've said, necessarily have an unsalable script on your hands if some of the ingredients of your script are not so good, or not as good as they might be. Exact perfection is for machines; it's rarely if ever achieved by man. The facts and techniques discussed in this book, however, are the means toward achieving the desirable and necessary satisfying *total* effect in your scripts, and I hope that you'll consider them carefully and use them wisely.

That about seems to cover it. Good luck. May all your troubles be little ones, and your royalty checks big ones.

Index

. . . says he's always mildly surprised to find himself visible as the author of a book, since he works mostly behind the scenes. He started out as a writer, however, selling his first story to a magazine at the age of fourteen, and had sold more than four hundred stories, serials, and articles before he was twenty-one. He also once undertook a contract with a small paperback publishing house and wrote nineteen novels for the firm in ten months.

Aside from *Writing to Sell,* of which the present book is the third revised edition, his favorite book among his own works is a biography, *George S. Kaufman and His Friends,* which was a best-seller, a Book-of-the-Month Club selection, excerpted in three magazines, republished in England even though Kaufman is little known there, and nominated for the Pulitzer Prize. He has also edited eleven anthologies (one of which, *The Fireside Treasury of Modern Humor,* is a thousand pages long), written the article on humor for three editions of the *Encyclopaedia Britannica* and the article on fiction for two editions of the *Oxford Encyclopaedia Britannica,* holds an honorary doctorate in letters, and appears occasionally as an expert witness in copyright cases and frequently on television and radio talk shows.

He lives on the north shore of Long Island with his wife, Helen, and they have a son, Steve, an M.D. and Ph.D. in Chicago, and a daughter, Randy, who is married to a young dentist in New York. The Merediths collect impressionist and post-impressionist art, and nearly every wall of their house is covered with paintings and drawings; even the kitchen area contains a Picasso, a Dali, a Magritte, a Laurencin, an Orozco, and a Dufy. They also collect netsuke, the little Japanese carvings in ivory and wood, and have one of the world's largest and most famous collections.